Are You There God?
Time To Eat Yet?

(A Book That Will Change the Way You Eat Forever)

By Lee Catalano
Boston

Dedication

This book is dedicated to every Soul who has experienced the mesmerism of food slavery, extra body weight and the imprisonment of the carnal mind.

Index

Introduction

This book will change the way you look at and relate to food forever. The answer is so simple, there are no diets, or rules of any kind. Within each of us is simple, clear direction from the wisdom of God within.

Each moment of every day we are choosing between the dictates of flesh and the freedom of spirit. Flesh and its wants and desires are driven by the carnal mind of the ego. All matters of spirit are inspired by God. One leads us to pain, suffering, sin, sickness and death. The other to perfection, happiness, The Garden of Eden and eternal life.

Carnal - adjective:

1. *pertaining to or characterized by the flesh or the body, its passions and appetites; sensual: carnal pleasures.*
2. *not spiritual; merely human; temporal; worldly: a man of secular, rather carnal, leanings.*

We can literally hear inspiration from God when we are still only for a moment. The more we remember to pause before eating, the more inspired and free we feel. Yes, I am literally writing about asking God what to eat. You will be surprised at what you hear. God will tell you what to eat for supper, lunch, breakfast, snack, dinner date, late-night snack, heartbreak nosh, celebration dinner, stress relief, party plate, business brunch, pub crawl, etc.

One of the most important things to acknowledge with weight loss, is choosing our food with the right mind. This means to get quiet for a moment and allow something else to come forward and do the choosing. There is no way to make peace with weight loss and food, without first learning to closely watch our minds. Once you've mastered the habit of mind watching, no longer abusing the body with food becomes natural.

"God's will for me is perfect happiness" states *A Course In Miracles*. God's will is perfect happiness and this is why it is so. There could never be a real will separate from God's, our falling into the mind of mortal thought has convinced us of another *false will*. This *false will* drives all of our bodily appetites and gives us the experience of separation from happiness, contentment and companionship.

Our temptation appears to be around food. The temptation that is driving our actions is within. It is no different than the temptation of Jesus on the desert during his 40 days and 40 nights of awakening. There is only one purpose of temptation and that is to keep you distracted from your inner light.

The only real companionship is in God. In that companionship we experience our relationship to others and everything more fully. In these pages are powerful ideas that will open you up to the Kingdom within you, where all of the answers are contained.

This is a book one can return to many times, to refresh the mind and reset direction. It is not just about weight loss, this book is helpful for breaking a spell of self-destruction of any kind. Addiction and sorrow, literally do not exist within the God-Vibe above carnal thought.

At age 52, I had tried many things both with success and not so much success, to lose weight and become trim. The easiest thing I have ever done in my life to maintain a healthy body size, was to have these four principles active in my mind. The principles are natural occurrences that come from being quiet for a moment throughout the day in true prayer, which is communion with God.

There is a larger dynamic going on than just food. Anyone who has tried to lose weight, or give up self-sabotage is well aware of this. There is a reality up above our thinking about food, and it's effects upon our bodies. Yes, the answer to food and addiction of any kind, is to give up all of our thought about it. One quiet moment at a time.

We will never be free from our inner demons through psychology of the world. I have left marriage counseling, depression counseling, etc., each time with more anxiety than when I arrived. Examining the carnal mind, with the carnal mind will never bring permanent relief.

Seeing and understanding the hypnotism of the carnal mind, and the willingness to let it go are key. Taking just one minute throughout the day to surrender "thy will be done not mine," releases us from bondage. The more often we remember, the more freedom from fear and anxiety we experience.

Ironically, these principles are not behavioral. They are automatic when we are communing with God throughout the day. You will find yourself only wanting food when you are actually hungry and okay with being a little hungry from time to time. You will also automatically find yourself asking within about food (*along with everything else*). The impulsiveness of the carnal mind cannot run the show when Self-awareness arises.

We will be delving more deeply into these four principles of eating with the mind of innocence. Enter into these pages with innocence in your mind and freedom in your heart. The time has come to put cause, true cause at the helm of your weight loss and feelings of well-being. The true cause IS God and His innocence and it's in your mind.

Within these pages the terms ego, carnal mind and serpent all mean the same thing. The darkness within the mind that wants us to suffer. I use them interchangeably in order to break down resistance.

Principles:

1. Know YOUR hunger cues.
2. Eat ONLY when hungry.
3. Eat as inspired.
4. Get inspired BEFORE you are hungry.

My entire family bounces right back to these principles should we find ourselves off of the rails with food. Adhering to, contemplating, and studying them leads to freedom with many things including food.

Food addiction is nothing more than the bondage of the carnal mind. We are incrementally rising above it. Food can be used as the threshold for awakening to the state of mind above the carnal mind's dictates.

Relaxing into your higher mind as little as one minute a few times per day plugs you into a state of mind where inspiration is given. Don't bother cleaning out your pantry. Just find a comfy corner, and free your mind.

Principle One: Know Your Hunger Cues

I have made it a study to ask people what their hunger cues are. Did you know that many people are not even aware of their hunger cues? What I learned is people who are naturally slim are not tempted to overindulge in food, and eat only when they're hungry. That said, everyone suffers at the hand of inner temptation of some kind. It is stated by the sages we unconsciously believe we are separate from God and therefore guilty and unworthy of God's perfect happiness. This is represented in the story of the Garden of Eden. The serpent is still whispering to us through the temptation of food. The temptation it holds before us is no longer the fruit of good and evil, it's our compulsive lust for food. The truth of us is God's perfection. We are finding our way back, one thought, one food choice at a time. We are leaving inner temptations behind and allowing ourselves to be lovingly guided.

With food at the end of our fingertips, and so readily available, we largely have lost touch with our inner hunger cues. We have learned to feed the body when we are bored, anxious, celebrating, sad, angry, tired and that is just the tip of the iceberg. The desire of the carnal mind for food, anchors us to its dictates.

For some, discovering what our hunger cues are can be a challenging task. Allowing yourself to become truly hungry can be fearful and daunting when we have not been experiencing this for many years, and for some of us, ever.

You will also be passing through all of the discomfort you were seeking relief from by over feeding the body. When you're passing through this phase, it feels as though it will last forever. It won't.

Remember when you stop listening to the ego's serpent dictates, it will kick up a lot of discomfort in order to get your attention back. If you go into this process knowing you are going to experience some temporary discomfort, you will have wonderful success!

Allow this phrase to become your mantra during the first 60 days while discovering your true hunger cues. "This Too Shall Pass." For some, the process will be instantaneous and for others (like me), it can be more intense for a period of time.

I myself, when going through this phase, have times in which I cry for no apparent reason. There is nothing in particularly bad going on in my life, it is the releasing of suppressed emotion. I also experience myself as irritable for absolutely no logical reason during the first two months.

After the first two months, as I begin getting comfortable, familiar and friendly with my hunger cues things got easier. I find I am not hungry for a significant amount of food until halfway through the day. I find my natural hunger cues are more of an experience of lightheadedness, than an actual growling in my stomach. Kelly's hunger cues are a growling tummy and lethargy. Robin's are nausea and stomach growling. Kelly and Robin are my grown daughters who live with me.

I began to experience the sweetness of life, which was not apparent before getting in touch with my hunger cues. Before discovering my hunger cues for the first time, I had not been a big eater, but I was eating a lot of extra bites of food here and there. I had started out at a size 10 and at the end of 2 months of simply finding my hunger cues, and eating along with the above mentioned principles, all of my clothes were loose and I felt great. What I discovered was when I eat only when hungry, food tastes much better than I ever could have anticipated. My experience of water became sweet, my appreciation for fruits, vegetables and all types of food increased and I have enjoyed food more than I ever have before.

Eating only when hungry takes self-hatred and guilt out of eating food. Which brings us to the **Principle Two.**

Principle Two - Eat ONLY When Hungry

Eating only when hungry sounds like a major buzz kill, but only to the ego/carnal mind, the truth of the matter is the opposite. When we eat for any reason other than hunger, we are depriving ourselves of self-love. When we are eating food for any other reason than to nourish the body, through inspiration, it is an act of self -hatred. This is HUGE, God's Will is for us to feel loved. We put ourselves in God's care around food by getting quiet and asking within. Yes, in the world we suffer a lot of dull aches, by *trying* to follow a will that is separate from God's. Not only is a will separate from God impossible, go within yourself and ask "who would *REALLY* want that?" God's will is not a buzz kill and will only ever elevate you, and whoever else enters your awareness. God's will covers ALL of the bases.

Keeping the truth in mind while learning of these four principles is vital. Do you believe that eating one extra bite of food when you are not hungry is self-hatred, and false temptation? Well if the effects of eating extra food are putting additional weight onto your body and adding aches and pains, I assure you it is self -hatred. You can know without a doubt which voice you are listening to when choosing your food, by how you feel.

When you decide through inspiration that you are going to eat only when hungry, you can go within and plan your day because now you know your hunger cues. If you have a particular occasion you can go within yourself and ask what will work best for you.

I found myself at the beginning of this process having a lot of freedom. In days gone by when I have gone on a diet, it always seemed dinner reservations increased. How many times have I gone to dinner and not been hungry, but ate anyway?

Initially, I felt fear experiencing hunger, in the beginning I had to watch my mind very closely for the first couple of months. Then I begin to be comfortable with the process. Now, I am perfectly comfortable allowing myself to get good and hungry. Oh yes, I have asked naturally slim people if they do this. Their response? "Oh yeah, the longer you wait the more awesome the food."

I went through the entire holiday season, I did not deprive myself of anything, and did not gain one pound. In fact, my clothes continued to loosen.

I often get caught up with life just like everyone else. The ego's biggest defense is unconsciousness. When we become unaware of what we are doing with food, we often find ourselves neck deep and disconnected. For me I often have no clue what I have been doing with food until my clothes start to get a little tight. Tight clothes are the cue for me to go back and become awake and aware of what I am doing with food. Yes, it's that simple.

It is vital to remember that using food for comfort is a big defense. What is it that we are seeking to be comforted from? The only discomfort we can possibly feel is from the carnal mind. Listening to the ego's dictates around food, are like asking a drug addict to hold onto our extra cash for us. We are suffering some sort of anxiety from our thinking, and then turn to the SAME mind for relief!

Once you know how to eat, the rest is easy peasy. Which leads into **Principle Three.**

Principle Three - Eat ONLY As Inspired

It is important to understand the process of forgiveness when eating as inspired. There are two very distinctly different things going on in the mind. Two different thought-systems. One is defined as the ego/carnal mind/serpent, I use them interchangeably in order to break down resistance. The other is the mind of innocence, also known as the Christ Mind/Right Mind/Buddha Mind. Forgiveness is looking beyond the temptation of thought from the carnal mind, and yes it IS a full-time job. Yours and my happiness are a full-time job.

The ego serpent in the mind is very compulsive and always speaks and chooses first around food (*and everything else*). What we are learning to do is to step back in our mind and allow something else to come forward. That something else that comes forward and does the choosing for us is the mind of innocence. When we take pause and choose with the mind of innocence, we never suffer. Remember, this is a journey, five steps forward, three back sometimes! Sometimes even six back! Hang in there, when the darkness passes you will find you have advanced through the false experience of darkness into more God-Vibe (happiness).

When first practicing to eat as inspired, I literally paused in the middle of the kitchen floor and went within. There were many times when I quieted my mind and knew a day ahead of time exactly what I would be eating the next day.

This is the process. I would sit in the chair, or be laying in my bed, be driving the car, or anywhere that I could be quiet and by myself. This is not a difficult, complicated process. I would relax my body, my shoulders, my arms, my neck, and allow everything within me physically to loosen. Then I would set my intention to go within myself and ask. I would approach the altar of food within and ask "what is it that would best nourlsh my body this meal?" I could literally shop, see, and pan the items in my fridge and pantry in my mind. It was very easy to receive the inspiration.

I find this process freeing. Not only was it helpful in stopping the attack upon the body with food, it was great to learn exactly what to eat, in order to feel good.

Learning to be inspired in the pantry awakens us to asking within in all aspects of life. We learn that asking within what to eat is a gift. We are literally developing the habit of knocking on God's door. God the Father in his purity, power, and perfection would never inspire us to harm ourselves.

I can see myself AVOIDING going within when the carnal mind wants what it wants. You know that feeling of not wanting to make eye contact when you KNOW you are choosing something that is not good for you? In the same way I find it very difficult to be quiet and go within when the carnal mind has taken over. When we have discomfort from listening to the wrong voice, consciously relaxing, nurturing ourselves and waiting for it to pass is key. "This too shall pass" is a practice of non-resistance, with the acknowledgement that we are off the rails. We KNOW there is a God and that power is quietly awaiting us to return to it.
This leads to **Principle Four.**

Principle Four - Get Inspired BEFORE You Are Hungry

I love this principle, it's a beautiful excuse to check-in with God. Getting inspired before you are hungry means knowing and having the assurance you have already gone within and know exactly what to do. When we are first becoming comfortable with these principles, we don't want to wait too long and find ourselves neck-deep in the pantry.

Another great thing about this principle is when you find yourself eating when not hungry, it's as simple as checking in before the next time you eat. I did not master this way of eating overnight. The simplicity of these four principles at first takes some time getting used to.

It's hard for the mind to grasp at first the simplicity of God and the ease of His answer.

After the first couple of months, you will find you can be inspired on the spot. Got that? You will have developed the habit of God.

The ego in the mind wants us to suffer, it will jump in at its first opportunity to make us forget that extra food means suffering. It is a good idea to have an ongoing relationship within, around food. Of course it's best for the purpose of not suffering to have this guidance in all things. If food is your cross, once you have mastered listening around food, the rest will be natural.

Another great title for this principle could be "don't eat (*or anything else*) before checking- in!!!"

Now for some inner spiritual principles to keep us on track...

Denial Of Feelings Of Shame

A Course in Miracles and many other spiritual Masters teach we are not our bodies. On every page of *A Course in Miracles* Jesus implores us to identify ourselves as pure, innocent, Souls. We are literally light (innocence), and when we are over feeding the body our experience of ourselves as Souls begins to deaden. The new testament of the Bible teaches us that we are not of this world. The carnal mind keeps us engaged in all things of this world, not the least of which is food and the size of the body. It has such a hold on us that we must become alert to it and its dictates in order to experience the perfection that is beneath all form. As our true identity, we are the perfection beneath all form. There is no compromise in this. We are the Christ, now we are becoming willing to experience ourselves as such.

Our feelings of shame go something like feeling disgusted when we are putting our clothes on, not wanting to have sex and be viewed naked by our partner, and so on. We become so far removed from the choices we are making in the pantry, they are miles away from our internal experience of our shame and feelings about our body. See that? Feelings of shame are always connected to the body. Ironically, when we turn our body over to the Voice of wisdom, everything is put in order.

Jesus asks us over and over in *A Course in Miracles* "how does it feel?" When we are feeling anything less than perfect happiness, we can be absolutely sure we are experiencing the effects of the listening to the compulsive carnal mind. Yes, it's time for us ALL (*especially me*) to learn to listen to the still, small, quiet Voice within. Perfect happiness comes from learning to listen to only one Voice in the manner which the Master Jesus did.

In the morning we look in the mirror, we don't like what we see in the mirror, we avoid making eye contact. Then we go about choosing our clothes, not from a place of play and innocence, but from a place of what will fit? Often times we feel like we would like to cry, but we push our feelings down, squish into our clothing, and move on with our day. We are so trapped by the mortal mind and its circular dictates we become unconscious.

Some spiritual people may say "I am NOT a body it doesn't matter what I eat." The carnal mind wants us to identify as sickly, painful bodies. Any time in our lives we have listened to the Voice of innocence within us, we did not suffer.

We have systematically conditioned ourselves in the experience of shame and its denial by continuously over feeding the body (*and many other of the carnal mind's dictates*). If we are waking up in the morning and looking in the mirror and squeezing into our clothes and feeling shame and disgust, we only need look back at the cause. Which voice in my mind have I been listening to when choosing food? There is a voice in our mind that speaks first in every situation in order to bring us an experience of sin, sickness and death (SHAME). When we learn to pause and listen to the still small Voice of love and innocence within the mind, we begin to experience freedom.

The carnal mind serves the body and its impulses, addictions, compulsions and shame. Jesus teaches us in *A Course in Miracles* and in the New Testament, the mind is split. This means that in between bouts of anxiety and shame, we do experience *degrees* of peace. We are literally conditioned to pain and shame. How do we know this? Anything other than perfect happiness, says Jesus, is not God's will for us. Only by listening to another *(false)* will, another voice in our minds, can we experience ourselves as shameful, guilty, and in pain.

When people lose weight too fast, without first healing their minds of shame and guilt, the weight loss cannot last. The reason the weight loss does not last? The mind is not ready to let go of suffering. It is important to not be in a hurry losing weight. Letting go and choosing again with the voice of innocence, is a slow, yet steady process.

Remember DENIAL is a BIG defense in the carnal mind's arsenal. It does NOT want you to "see" its shenanigans.

We all know what it feels like to awaken the next day after a day of "clean" eating. We feel light and good! THAT is what we are learning to adjust to...feeling good. We tell ourselves that we feel good because the weight is off of our body, because we are a smaller size. The truth is we feel better because we are no longer carrying the effects of the carnal mind, we are learning to listen less and less. The weight loss is simply an effect.

The Carnal Mind Always Speaks First Around Food

If you really believed there was a voice in your mind that wanted you dead would you choose more carefully around food? Jesus tells us in *A Course in Miracles* the ego wants us dead. Reason would tell me that anytime I'm choosing with the ego I will surely suffer.

Remember the serpent in the Garden of Eden? It was all perfection in the Garden of Eden and the serpent wanted man to eat from the tree of good and evil. Now what is man continuously doing? Looking at all bodies and judging good and evil. Out of perfection, *higher mind,* we went into continuous judgment, *lower mind.* Higher mind with God = heaven, lower mind carnal = hell (nothingness).

You can clearly see the effects of choosing with the carnal mind in the world. Extra weight on the body leads to painful knees, hips, and all sorts of modern day illness. When we choose with the wrong voice in the pantry its effects are evident, if we are willing to see.

Can you think of another area of life in the world where choosing with the carnal mind leads to things going terribly wrong? Perhaps our love lives, finances, career? It's all the same and I have no doubt you can give several examples of these circumstances. I know I can!

No one is a compulsive overeater, they *(we)* are just unconsciously responding to the compulsive thought in mind. The carnal mind says *"Choose now quickly! Suffer later! (unconscious effects)"* When we take pause, the still small voice that will only lead us to happiness, can come forth and do the choosing. Repeatedly, in *A Course In Miracles* Jesus teaches us to apply reason to the choices we make. I know for me a lot of the time I don't see the error I took in my mind until AFTER I have taken a wrong turn. That is okay! Forgiveness (looking beyond) in the rear view mirror is better than no forgiveness at all!

You can see this mechanism of compulsion in the mind at work in other areas of your everyday life. The compulsion in the mind is what tempts us to judgment with every encounter we have. If we are completely honest with ourselves, we can see that we are tempted to a judgment every single time we encounter a brother. Those who have learned to be gentle around others and offer a blessing, have learned to ignore (forgive) the compulsion of judgement. This compulsive mind also reveals itself when we are anxious for someone to finish talking so we can speak.

When you first start allowing yourself to go within, and experience inspired eating, you will continuously forget what you chose. Learning to still your mind and still your body for a moment and choose with the Voice of innocence takes commitment. In the beginning it can be difficult, I'm not going to tell you it's always easy.

When you make a commitment and you KNOW there will be challenges, you will remain focused and able to meet resistance. The serpent within WILL rise up with resistance, but it won't last forever. This resistance will show up as forgetfulness. Just take a moment and search your mind for the choice you have already made for food.

"The ego IS an ally of time, but NOT a friend. For it is as mistrustful of death as it is of life, and what it wants for you, IT cannot tolerate. The ego wants YOU dead, but NOT itself. The outcome of its strange religion MUST therefore be the

conviction that it can pursue you BEYOND the grave. And out of its unwillingness for you to find peace, even in the death it WANTS for you, it offers you immortality in hell. It speaks to you of Heaven, but assures you that Heaven is not for you. How can the guilty hope for Heaven?" A Course In Miracles

You see? Where is the ego? It's in your mind and we are choosing between it and the Voice for life every minute of every day. We can learn to choose again and be free around food. The ego always speaks first, but there is something else, all we need to do is learn to listen to it. We take pause, we go within and listen.

When I first started living by these 4 principles, I found myself habitually reaching for snacks and bites of food that my body did not need. One night in particular, I got a phone call with bad news. I noticed as soon as I hung up the phone I robotically walked over and opened the refrigerator. As I stood in front of the refrigerator I was watching myself looking the food up and down. I was searching my mind for the inspired direction I had received earlier. It was not there, I could not pull forward what it was I had been inspired to eat. It was fascinating watching my compulsive mind on automatic pilot. It just so happened I was not hungry and I closed the refrigerator. About a half an hour later I was walking past my dresser and saw a snack bar *(I had put there when inspired)*. It was amazing first observing the compulsion when stressed and then completely going numb to the inspiration. It passed, that is what I learned, it passes.

Choose Once Again (In your mind and therefore the pantry!)

Choose Once Again

"Temptation has one lesson it would teach, in all its forms, wherever it occurs. It would persuade the Holy Son of God he is a body, born in what must die, unable to escape its frailty, and bound by what it orders him to feel. It sets the limits on what he can do; its power is the only strength he has; his grasp cannot exceed its tiny reach. Would you BE this, if Christ appeared to you in all His glory, asking you but this, "Choose once again if you would take your place among the Saviors of the world, or would remain in hell, and hold your brothers there." For He HAS come, and He IS asking this." A Course In Miracles.

There is splendor inside of each and every one of us. We mistakenly think it is no big deal to be unconscious around food. When we are unconsciously choosing our food, or choosing to escape our current state of mind, we are choosing self-destruction. We are seeking relief within the same thought system that is bringing us discomfort. Taking pause, and choosing again in the pantry, is literally life changing. The circular experience of food compulsion, coming from the carnal mind, is keeping us in darkness.

It's vital that we stay awake and aware and remember how wonderful we feel when we choose rightly, with the mind of God. This is what *choosing once again* means, it means literally choosing with God and no longer choosing with carnality. One wants to lead us to green everlasting pastures, and the other wants to nail us on the cross.

What does it look like to be nailed on the cross with food? It feels like shame, embarrassment, no sense of self-worth, diminished sex drive, feelings of depression, low energy, extra body weight, aches and pains, and the list goes on. It is vital to remember, this is exactly how carnality within wants you to experience yourself. It wants you to believe that you are less-than, ghoulish, freakish and not good enough.

When you come back to these words and are ready to step away from your denial, seeing the inner serpent will stop you in your tracks. Freedom is as close as your next choice. I know I continuously forget in order to remember in a more lasting way.

The two thought systems, are representative of two very different self-identities. The carnal mind keeps us locked into the little identity, the little self. When we take pause and choose with the Voice for Love, we become more closely identified with our Soul. Soul identification is happy, free, healthy, bouncy and generous in all ways. When we feel good we want to give ourselves away. It just is what it is. We all know how it feels to want to pull the covers up and not answer the door. That feeling will never come from listening to the Voice for Love. That Voice knows the Soul gives itself away in unending love, patience, kindness and abundance. The body then becomes a vital tool for communicating happiness.

Being a mother, what comes to mind for me is the child coming home from school with the drunken parent on the sofa. The parent cannot get out of their own way, they have been listening to the carnal voice of the little self. We become slave to the carnal mind without awareness of another choice. That voice makes the darkness of the world go round and wants us on the sofa fat, sad, hungover and miserable.

We are here in a process of "choose once again." That means spiritual wisdom KNOWS this is a process. The more we choose with our higher mind, the better we feel. We are not getting used to skinnier bodies, we are getting acclimated with feeling good! When we choose less with the carnal mind, all things begin to be set right.

The Hypnotism Of Food

There is nothing bad, or shameful about being hypnotized by food. The world is very purposefully hypnotizing us with it's advertising and temptation. We are not wrong in being circular in our pain, frustration, and the shame that has come upon us through food. We oftentimes don't want to see what it is we are doing because we feel guilty. We fear looking within and seeing what we are doing, because we are SO sure we are going to find ourselves wanting. Then what happens when we find ourselves wanting? How do we change?

The very first step out of hypnotism is knowing that you are hypnotized. The spell of using food to comfort, and suppress our feelings runs deep. What are we so afraid of? What if the spells were broken? What would be left without the hypnotism?

I remember quitting smoking, the first thing that happened, I became acutely aware of what I was doing with cigarettes. I allowed myself to smoke as much as I wanted to. I first went through a phase of really seeing what I was doing, how much I was smoking and when. The first thing I noticed was that I largely smoked unconsciously.

I began to smoke consciously and only when I was well aware of what I was doing. My favorite time to have a cigarette was standing by my window, talking on the phone, taking a ten minute break from domesticity and my kids. I can remember now standing in the window. It was chin high with fresh air coming in. I had many laughs smoking those cigarettes, making smoke rings and blowing out the window.

I allowed myself to continue smoking. As I began to really observe, I started tasting the chemicals moving over my tongue. Without depriving myself, or making myself wrong, I began to get grossed out by cigarettes. I even switched to organic cigarettes, hoping they would taste better. I naturally reduced to 2 cigarettes per week. I remember a doctor telling me that it was no big deal to smoke 2 cigarettes per week, I also remember feeling like the doctor was full of s*** because I could not run the way I wanted to. I knew the cigarettes were holding me back.

When you become aware of, and stop denying that a behavior is an act of self-hatred, the behavior begins to loosen. In my experience, looking straight on at a compulsion is the beginning of the end. This is why we are so resistant to looking within. The mind that drives the compulsion will throw up any excuse to keep us from looking because it is the beginning of ITS end.

As much as I THOUGHT I enjoyed smoking, looking it right in the eye was the beginning of the end of it. I quit smoking many years ago.

With food the hypnotism is in thinking we are doing something to relieve ourselves, help ourselves. We are hypnotized by beautiful, sweet, luscious food. Food is literally advertised to appeal to our carnal, lustful desires. When you look at food that is oozing sweet sauce and topped off with creamy sweetness, you are being hypnotized. The last thing on our minds is nourishment of the body and soul. Anytime that we eat without deep gratitude for food and God, it is self-hatred.

How often are we driven to the snack bar at the movie theater, or drive-ins? Are we sitting in the dark movie eating robotically? Or are we in deep gratitude for nourishing the body? These are not questions to ask oneself and evoke guilt or shame. These are questions that will break the hypnotic spell of eating unconsciously, and bringing the experience of self-hatred.

The thing is, once we are snapped out of hypnotism, we can't believe we were ever hypnotized. We first have to see that we are hypnotized and our conviction keeps us more and more clear minded.

Food And Self-Hatred

I remember walking down the sidewalk and literally wincing when glancing at myself in a window. I was so filled with shame. I didn't call it that, I would just push down the discomfort and keep it moving. I had NO CLUE that I was experiencing these feelings as an effect of listening to a dark cause in my mind. I was choosing foods that were making me sick and NEVER eating when hungry. I was so far removed from any true hunger cues, the concept was foreign and scary.

Here I was terrified of hunger and trying to go on a diet! Common sense will tell anyone how long that is going to last!

BEFORE you go on any food plan, doesn't it make sense to get comfortable with your hunger cues? When I started losing weight, the weirdest thing to adjust to was the lack of self- hatred. When we carry around extra weight along with all of its effects, we have suffered for a long time. NOT SUFFERING then takes getting used to. One can baulk every day all day at what I am saying, but this IS the reason people put the weight right back on. It comes off too fast and they feel a strange anxiety. Not suffering is unfamiliar.

"You do not want to suffer. You may think it buys you something, and may still believe a little that it buys you what you want. Yet this belief is surely shaken now, at least enough to let you question it, and to suspect it really makes no sense. It has not gone as yet, but lacks the roots that once secured it tightly to the dark and hidden secret places of your mind." A Course In Miracles

I used to think, until recently actually, that there were two wills. God's will and then the relinquishment of mine. I really thought that I knew better and surrendering my ideas would definitely be a bummer. This could absolutely not be further from the truth. There is only one true will and that IS God's will. The term "God's will" has been so diminished and perverted by religion it takes more than a moment to relax into it.

Perverted - (of a thing) having been corrupted or distorted from its original course, meaning, or state.

When we listen to the Voice for Love within us we could NEVER experience self- hatred. I recently had a conversation with my friend Zoe about listening to the Voice for Love around food for ONE DAY. She was talking about waking up and feeling so good. What happens when we become more comfortable with stringing several days together? The miracles of innocence and happiness, that is what happens. We feel it within so powerfully we become the medium of God's miracles.

Letting go of self- hatred is a vibrational journey. KNOW that you are RIGHT ON track even when you fall off of the rails. This is the truth! Don't be afraid to observe your mind and how you feel.

The steel door (in our minds) that has us baulk at the thought of self-hatred, is DENIAL.

"I share God's Will for happiness for me, and I accept it as my function now." A Course In Miracles

Dethroning The Wrath Of God By Crucifying Ourselves First!

Time for a deep delve into Spiritual Psychology. This is so huge. Learning what the ego's shenanigans are about is vital to breaking a spell (hidden false belief). I spoke earlier about the perversion of God in religion. It's not the religion, we have to widen our observation and go back to the effect driving the religion. Did you go there? Yup, lid is off, someone at the helm was listening to the voice of the carnal mind. The carnal mind wants every Soul to believe there is a wrathful God outside of us looking to punish us.

The whole story of the ego/carnal mind's thought system is evident in religion. "You are bad and guilty, God is going to get you! Repent!"

The ego/serpent in our mind has us unconsciously believing if we suffer at our own hand we are defeating God, according to A Course In Miracles.

The ego tells us that we have abandoned God, he is viciously angry and will strike us down if we go within. Remember this is all unconscious, but if we pay close attention to our actions, we will see that it is true. It's all about the unconscious self-sabotage baby. Well the light is going ON!

It is only by going within that we can see/perceive which voice we have been listening to. The ego/serpent in your mind wants you suffering. The ego voice IS suffering. Got that, the world is literally run by a thought-system of pain and suffering.

Can you feel it right now? Is any part of your body tense, or clenching? Any thought that would cause you to clench or hold tension is not God's Will. We have work to do. Don't feel bad about it, be glad that you are beginning to see/perceive.

The world is convinced it must suffer. This is why we call our friends and family members when we are suffering, we ARE abiding in a will, but it is not God's. Are you ready to stop telling people how bad it is? This is a powerful upliftment towards God's vibration, simply stopping yourself from speaking words of suffering is an enormous shift into a higher state of mind.

In *A Course In Miracles* Jesus tells us he is not concerned with our actions. He is concerned with our THINKING because it drives our actions. Speaking is an action. What mind (*carnal or inspired*) is driving our words, and therefore our actions?

Feeling anything but pure love and acceptance for ourselves and others is to be in the state of crucifixion (*carnal mind*). How many times after a holiday, or birthday dinner did I just want to be alone to languish in my over-full belly and self- hatred?

Sometime after having my son, I began to slim down. I clearly remember standing in the kitchen and having this feeling that the other shoe was going to drop. I was SO uncomfortable. Deep down I did not feel worthy of feeling GOOD. This is why many lose weight and become alcoholics, or have affairs. With my high-risk pregnancy, I had gained 90 lbs. Much of it was water, 50 lbs of it was pure, toxic fat. I had divorced while pregnant and used food to further punish myself. My life had become unmanageable across the board, and having a skinny waist line was not going to fix it. My thinking needed an overhaul and by overhaul I mean I needed to give it up. I was pissed, hurt, angry and needed to give it up, forgive my thinking. It was ALL the carnal mind and my listening to it that was making me SUFFER.

If we do not practice forgiveness we will surely find another way in which to SUFFER and bring chaos to our threshhold (*mind*). We cast out one demon (*false belief*) and make room for six more. Suffering is NOT God's will and therefore not ours either. Remember we are doing nothing more or less than forgiving (looking beyond) the compulsive thoughts of the carnal mind.

We are taught through the spiritual doctrine of *A Course In Miracles* that using the body as anything other than a communication device is projection. When we overfeed the body we inevitably end up caught in a circular web of self- hatred and thoughts of self-abasement. If we ACT as though we are weak egos that are in need of comfort, we will FEEL like weak egos in need of comfort. The ego is in need of comfort and it cannot BE comforted. Therefore its credo is *"seek and do not find."* This is only within it's thought system. Relief is found within, up above the thinking mind.

It is impossible to detach ourselves from the CAUSE of our actions. Every word we speak, every action we take, is from the Bread Of Life, or from the voice of sin, sickness and death. There is no compromise in this. I am not saying these words in order to scare you, I am saying these words in order to awaken you and me. It is also vital to be gentle with ourselves and to understand it takes time to turn the ship of mind around. We go five steps forward, and then sometimes six steps back. Nothing has gone wrong. Remember to go back to the principles and to be kind to yourself. For YOU are sacred and where you sit, stand, and speak RIGHT NOW is sacred ground. It is time for the self- hatred to end. My arm is around your shoulder, we are heading for the door to freedom.

Dieting

Dieting is penance, it is no change at all. Dieting is an act of self-punishment, in order to make up for something you have done wrong. It is more of the same. When you look in the mirror and say to yourself that you need to lose weight, you are so far off the rails from cause, and the ego wants you that way. By that I mean you are looking to the same thought system that is *causing* you pain.

What part of you would look at your body and think "I need to lose weight?" How does a thought like that make you feel? I'll tell you how it makes me feel...TERRIBLE. It is the instant way to feel unacceptable and trapped. Nothing like the thought "I need to lose weight" to send a girl back to the fridge for more comfort! You KNOW it's true!

Here is the rhythm of dieting. You feel like holy hell and decide to do something about it. So you go to the store and get all the right foods, you buy new sneakers, you are committed. You are eating foods you likely don't eat, in a manner you don't normally eat, and are aware every day you are paying a penance *(for being fat)*. The first couple of days you feel good and then the dinner invitation comes in. It only takes a couple of dinner invitations to blow our diet because we were not really digging it in the first place. What comes to mind is the old adage "I went on a diet and gained ten lbs."

Allow yourself to thoroughly observe what you are doing with food without changing a thing. Stop allowing guilt to drive your actions. You CAN say to yourself "Hmmm which voice/Voice have I been listening to around food?" Then get yourself back to the four principles. STAT.

Needing to lose weight and diets are NOT of the Voice for God. Do you feel like a bait and switch just happened? You are right, one did, we are doing no less than turning a whole entire thought system on its ear. Extra toxic weight falls off as a result of no longer listening to extra, toxic thought. No diets here. EVER.

To Teach Is To Demonstrate

To Teach is To Demonstrate

"To teach is to demonstrate. 2 There are only two thought systems, and you demonstrate that you believe one or the other is true all the time. 3 From your demonstration others learn, and so do you. 4 The question is not whether you will teach, for in that there is no choice. "- A Course In Miracles

It's very easy for me to look at this quote and think about what I am teaching others. The deeper message contained within it, is I am teaching myself and others simultaneously all of the time. It *would* be hilarious to think we have people fooled *(into thinking we are happy)* when we are living deeply steeped in the ego's thought system and carrying extra weight. It WOULD be, but for the suffering.

I have had people ask me if I am in love because I am a naturally happy person. Yes, I am deeply in love, but not with ONE body walking around the world. I am moving more and more into the experience of feeling exquisite love with each and every encounter. I sometimes have to stick my finger nail into a nail bed to keep from crying at an inappropriate time. Often times people are speaking words that have NOTHING directly to do with God and all I hear is God and I get tears. The other day I felt so moved while walking through Harvard Square I HAD to step into a church so I could cry freely.

Happiness and purity have an image in the world and that image is you and me, me and you. God appearing as the Christ and communicating through the body. This IS the Bread of Life that feeds us, truly feeds us.

God And Forgiveness
(yes, I am going there)

Genesis 2:17

"But from the tree of the knowledge of good and evil you shall not eat, for in the day that you eat from it you will surely die."

God is above the duality of good and evil. God goes about replenishing the earth after a fire because there is no thought to block His perfection. There is only perfection in God. WE took on the belief of good and evil, it did NOT come from God. Yes, I am talking about form, and not resisting the God-Vibe that is beneath all form. We are the same as the trees and life coming back after fire. When we are not resistant to and blocking God, perfection comes forth. God was all that occupied the mind of the Master Jesus and all were healed in his presence. He brought the God-Vibe of perfection into the world. We are being called to do the same.

At this very moment in my mind I am turning any thoughts of this body over to God. I am telling God thank you. I am going to write my prayer, first I am searching my mind for any grievance I may be holding. I wait and the one, or ones come forward in my mind. It is easy to let go a grievance because holding one was always the result of a deep, dark spell in my own mind. THERE IS ONLY PERFECTION IN GOD and my experience of anything other than that is my own error. Seeing another as a body and believing in the actions of the carnal mind, is the biggest error of all.

Eye closed with prayer hands:

Grievances:
Nothing has gone wrong, nothing has gone wrong, I am blessed by you and in God's name I would know of your blessings. You are blessed by me and I by you. Thank you. Nothing has gone wrong there is no evil here...only perfection. Repeat with as many that come to mind.....

True Prayer is always communion with God:
Thank you Father for I am in you and you within me. You are the Greater, the Creator and I am your Son. Dwelling within me is you, I am yours, thank you Father. I am not Fatherless; I share the one Father with my sacred brothers equally. We are one and the

ground we walk is sacred. The words we speak are your Bread of Life. I hear your words come forth from my brothers all day long. I have the ears you have given me in order to hear your word. Thank you Father. Amen.

Living by these four principals is an opportunity for further communion with God. It's not about asking God for stuff, it's about communing with God and as a result of that communion, knowing how to eat.

Prayer is the medium of miracles, it denies the denial of Truth. Nothing in God could ever go wrong. We are in God. Amen.

The habit of true prayer is a gift to ourselves. We learn, feel and live in God's Will. God's Will is ONLY perfection! Who doesn't want perfection at the wheel?

Thank you God. In you I have been perfected! Amen! See? How does that make you feel? Pray it, speak it, FEEL it. Then allow your own words of truth to come. If you only receive one thought, repeat it!

Anxiety And Diet Change

When we are letting go of the compulsion to food and listening to the mind of suffering, we are letting go a HUGE defense. First, I want to think about what it is I have been defending against. For me to reach for extra food would mean there is something internal that I am not feeling comfortable with. Taking in extra food suppresses every single bodily function and slows us down. What am I trying to dull down?

What if all of this suppression of emotion is dulling down my connection with God? Hmmm now there is a big wake up call. When my body is working hard I am very aware of it. When my tummy is too full it becomes bloated and I feel like I have concrete in my intestines. This is not a state of neutrality. Worth repeating: THIS IS NOT A STATE OF NEUTRALITY.

We are taught in *A Course In Miracles* that the ego/serpent and the Mind of Christ/Love are mutually exclusive. We absolutely cannot be experiencing them at the same time. The effects of either one, are as near as our next thought. Jesus teaches in *ACIM* that the ego feels very threatened when it is not being utilized in our mind. What does that look like when we are stepping away from it's compulsive dictates with food? TEMPTATION (carnal).

When temptation was knocking at the door of my mind I could feel it as a physical sensation. This sensation felt like terrible anxiety. The thing about anxiety is that when you are in it, in NO WAY do you feel it is going to pass.

The thought is "this too shall pass away" reminds us of the temporary nature of mental, emotional chaos. Anxiety is pretty rare for me now, but when it does come, this is my "go to" thought. Not adding any thought to your state of mind and going into soothing mode is vital. The thought "this too shall pass" circumvents the anxiety and when you start soothing yourself it falls away. For me? There is no day that is not made a little better with a re-run of Magnum PI. What soothes you? A ball game? A walk? A phone conversation (don't talk about your anxiety!)? Painting your nails? Music? Just like we tried *(miserably)* with the food, go within and learn to truly sooth yourself, food is not soothing, it's numbing.

Anxiety passes, when not fed (literally) and cannot sustain itself. We must add fearful thought in order to keep it going. I know what I am talking about with anxiety. I suffered from agoraphobia, depression and anxiety attacks as a young woman. Feeling the anxiety and feeding it fear thoughts puts us in circular terror. Who wouldn't want to eat just for relief? Have your healing thought *(this too shall pass)* ready in your mind. Anxiety WILL hit and you WILL be ready.

2 Corinthians 4: 17-18 "For our present troubles are small and won't last very long. Yet they produce for us a glory that vastly outweighs them and will last forever. So we don't look at the troubles we can see now; rather, we fix our gaze on things that cannot be seen. For the things we see now will soon be gone, but the things we cannot see will last forever."

Anxiety is a defense risen by the ego in order for it to get and hold your focus on it. Always remember, the serpent IS anxiety. Unless we are listening to the Voice for Love within us, we are experiencing some level of anxiety. At times it's barely detectable, but it's there. The carnal mind wants you to eat in a manner that *causes* pain and anxiety.

If you look back at your life you can clearly see when things were going well the anxiety level could get out of control. We get the awesome job, handsome fun dude, or dudette, start losing weight and what happens. Anxiety UP! In your happiness the serpent knows you are gone from it's clutches and will throw up everything it can in order to get you back to utilizing its thoughts. It tells you that you are not good enough, you don't belong and you are basically a freak show. All of these wonderful, and bountiful things are the fruits of God. They are your inheritance and the Tree of Life will never run out of fruit. God is always giving, our natural function is always giving.

Truth? Um, you were created in perfection and you tell me where it is that you could possibly not belong? You have a light in you so bright and God himself (the very center of your being) wants you to shine it wherever it is that you find yourself. Got that? Good!

When I put down extra bites of food I had all kinds of anxiety, it skyrocketed, but only for a short time. I remember about 5 days in ... crying off and on all day long! I stood in the living room window home alone at night and cried. This is not typical for me! I was observing myself cry over literally nothing. You and I both know how easy it would be to add some sort of bummer in the world to add to my tears. I have all kinds of sad material available in my mind just like everyone else in the world. I was NOT going there! Guess what? It passed.

The thing with anxiety is this...when you are feeling it you absolutely do not believe it will pass. Watching our minds very closely will set us free. I am feeling a prayer coming on:

Thank you Father, for in you I am made whole and complete. There is no opposite in your perfection. I am yours, thank you Father, I am yours. The Father and I are one, for He is greater, yet I abide in Him. Thank you for your perfection and in that am I. Thank you God, thank you One Father. Thank you. Amen.

Resistance

The serpent within is not going to gently pack it's bags and leave your awareness. When the ego feels you have been somewhere else and it no longer has you like it used to, LOOK OUT! Things starting to go your way? This is when you lose your keys, get in a fender bender, have a stupid argument about nothing, lose money and so on.

Remember when I said above, "I went on a diet and gained ten pounds." Something like that. The world is literally run by the ego and its insecurities. You know when you feel like you are not good enough? Well, that is not you, it's the serpent within. *A Course In Miracles* teaches us that whatever makes us miserable is delight for the ego. Think about that for a minute. I mean REALLY ponder it. What does it mean to you? To me it means something is alive and well and feeding off of my misery when I can't fit into my pants, or my mind is stuck in thoughts of feeling like a "Large Marge."

Resistance can show up like aches and pains, excuses and a whole lot of sneaky things. How do we know which way to go when we have decided we want to listen to the Voice within? What do we do when we really really don't FEEL like listening? I always defer to this one inner question. When I was at peace what did I decide? Yup, that is the way to roll, whatever it is that inspired you while at PEACE, not what you are thinking in a whiny, tired moment.

Resistance will also show up as forgetfulness BIG TIME. The egos largest defense is for us to forget what and why we are listening to the Voice within. Once we are caught up in the ego's thought system of sloth, it is easy to forget because IT doesn't think inspired thoughts!

I have gone for periods of time, days and weeks on end with my nose in spiritual doctrine and contemplation. I have experienced vertigo BIG TIME as a result of my determined focus. Remember, THIS TOO SHALL PASS. It does.

Prayer:

You and I are joined within the magnificence of God in His eternal perfection and beauty. Amen.

Communion With God

We are taught in spiritual doctrine to "seek ye first the Kingdom of Heaven and all things will be added." Okay, but what does that mean in everyday life? The place to seek Heaven is in prayer and contemplation. We develop a habit of prayer and remembering.

Once we have caught the buzz of God we want more. I laugh to myself as I type that thought, because it is so true of anything that makes us feel better. When the thoughts of God and His purity and perfection are in the forefront of the mind, other things begin to fall away. We are literally getting used to and familiar with the vibration of God. Anything and everything else has been a nightmare of our own making.

What we are doing with food begins in thought, or should I say mis-thought. We are lifting false gods between us and God. What are false gods? Thoughts and therefore compulsions and judgments.

We no longer need to worry about the size of our body, and add thoughts of self- hatred to all of that. Can you see how thoughts of raising the body up,

OR throwing ourselves down are all the same? You don't have to worry about that meaning the body is not real, and therefore being huge is your destiny. Being happy, radiant and free is your destiny and it is God's Will and therefore your Will as well. Say that fast three times. Lol.

Invoke your mind in communion within, what would a radiant child of God (you) look like? How would God have you look? Who knows right? What a beautiful place of surrender and discovery to be in the care of God the Father Himself.

There is a way we feel when we are immersed in the world with food compulsion, which IS ego-thought compulsion. There is another way we feel when we are immersed in spirit above compulsion. We are literally getting conditioned back to our true state of being. Perfection is so far from how we experience ourselves right now. This is actually good news!

We are worthy of so much more than we have given ourselves!

I was speaking to my daughter Robin this morning. Robin has been drinking smoothies and is feeling amazing. I can see her glowing and she looks amazing. We were talking about the two ways in which to see her transformation. One way is to be concerned about and have an eye on a goal of weight loss. Robin pointed out to me that she is feeling closer to God than ever, and that is very different from how she was feeling carrying extra weight and eating unconsciously.

We all know how this goes. With just one simple shift in goal, the path is revealed all shiny and new. The goal is communion with God. There are only happiness and good things in God.

Everything that you can possibly imagine or see has its beginning in thought. Life becomes magical in all areas when we are no longer blocking the thoughts of God, which come from direct communion and inspiration.

We are the ones on the planet who will demonstrate the beatific realms of life through communion with God. Extra food in the body is a block to that communion and why on Heaven and Earth would we want to do that? The answer is we wouldn't. God's Will is our Will, we have just been long deceived by a voice within that has us focused on everything but.

There is no hurry in this so remember to take it easy on yourself. Our vibe will rise incrementally and that is the exact way it is supposed to. Many will read my words and a switch will flip for them in order to never go back to taking an extra bite of food again. Others will need an on-going process, a little going back and forth for a bit (like me). All of this is in perfect order.

If Jesus teaches in *A Course In Miracles* that egos don't love or join, it has surely been a sad state of affairs in the world. Are we ready for LOVE? The real deal? The kind of love that can never leave and all we have to do is raise prayer hands in order to remember. Are we ready to recognize that any love we have ever felt has always been God? Any kindness ever offered has always been God through your brother? Yup, it's all God and we can have as much of it as we desire. Love is literally here and there, but for our taking. Can you freakin imagine that?!

The compulsive mind within that is choosing first in the pantry does NOT want you connecting with God. In your connection with God is the end of suffering and the end of it. One day soon we will say "I was looking to lose a few pounds and ended up in the Kingdom of Heaven!"

You don't have to be a meditator, or do anything ceremoniously. Just put your hands together and take a moment to pray. You will find at first you are doing it in private, then you will grow to praying with no self consciousness at any time. Pray out loud in front of those you love, demonstrate what true prayer is: COMMUNION WITH GOD ONLY. Now you most certainly need not pray in front of anyone. Prayer in private is powerful.

EVEN IF we are having a off day and don't want to commune with God over food or anything else, do it consciously. It's okay, tell God you will be back tomorrow, next week, in a decade, just be aware! Nothing has ever gone wrong and we are innocent no matter what.

Prayer:

Thank you Father, in your light I am never alone. You have created me to be your companion in perfection. Thank you Father Thank you Father for your bread of Life that flows freely from my brother every moment of every day. I am yours and your will is mine. I breathe your breath, I speak your words, I walk on your Holy, sacred ground. Amen.

Sacredness And God's Will

In my arrogance I really thought, first that there were two wills and second, that mine was WAY more fun than God's. Here is the deal with God's Will. God is above good and evil in a vibe that is of purity and perfection. Got that? PURITY AND PERFECTION. What have I ever done that could not have been made better by God? Wow this just hit me as a deep question. Who would I have married, or not married?

In my life I have run so many agendas that were a separate will from God's. A miserable made-up will that is. I wanted to feel wanted by someone and we all know how that goes. Without the Grace of God's Will we are hanging in the balance of good and evil and at its relentless mercy. My first book is an intense journey through the end of that in my life.

You and I are sacred, just take a moment and be with that thought for a moment. I am going to pray.

Prayer:

Thank you Father for you have created me in your sacred image. I am yours and you are the only thing that is true about me. I feel your sacredness within me, I am nourished in your sacredness with every bite of food, with every sip of drink, with every word I speak. Amen.

Food is sacred in God, but for our remembering. Everything is sacred in God, if you are reading, or writing this book you need a little help remembering the sacredness of food. The thing is, the sacredness of food never goes away. It's not like we blow a diet and gain a million pounds because we forgot for a moment, it has nothing to do with that. Food is sacred and when we remember, it is more delicious and satisfying than ever. Everything is sacred and I am moving into that EXPERIENCE through food. My former cross is becoming a vehicle to experiencing the God within.

Ask yourself: is it sacred to weigh, measure and count calories? Or is it edging God and His Love out? I'm not telling anyone to stop that, I am just opening a door of mind for self- inquiry. Never be afraid to question why we do what we do. It's a vital step in awakening to our power in God's purity. Many feel good when they have a discipline they do not stray from, it helps keep denial at bay. Whatever gets one through the night. If discipline helps, I say "bravo" and follow your inspiration.

John 6:35
Jesus said to them, "I am the bread of life; he who comes to Me will not hunger, and he who believes in Me will never thirst."

Reading the words that tell us we are sacred are helpful because it opens our minds. Practicing the sacred by remembering God is the medium of miracles. A miracle is where destruction of carnal thought has been replaced by gentleness and understanding.

Pray truly for union with God and nothing else. The rest will be taken care of, you will find that you are inspired in a way to eat that can never harm and only heal. Why? Because you are sacred and you are in the care of the Father who adores and does nothing but perceive your sacredness all through eternity.

Have you ever thought of yourself in terms of sacred? How would you treat someone whom you believed was sacred? Many lose their minds over having visions of mother Mary. You are the same in your sacredness as mother Mary. Did you know that?

It makes no difference how anyone has ever treated you in your life. I suffered more humiliation than you can shake a stick at. All false. No one can define you in this world because you are not of this world. Remember the statement from our brother Jesus that he was not of this world? Well he wanted you and me to see ourselves like him; joined with him in the Father. We are not of this world either! This world, and belief in it as a real and solid place that defines you, or anyone, is just cruel. You were created by the Father and equal to every sacred Soul in this world and out of it.

You can't get to the feeling of sacred with your body's eyes, you have to go within. Sacred has no form, it is spirit. You and I are spirit, that spirit animates these bodies. Our sacredness never left the realm of spirit and became a body, we still exist within the realm of sacred spirit.

Taking a moment throughout the day to raise your hands in true prayer to God is literally phoning home,

it's calling your Father who loves you. Who doesn't want that? We have been so long mistaken about what true prayer is. It's phoning home! *ET had it straight all along (reference to movie ET).*
So I study this and I study that. I listen to this one and go on retreats with that one. What am I doing in everyday life? Am I phoning home to the sacred in order to remember my sacredness?

Mathew: "Jesus answered, "It is written: 'Man shall not live on bread alone, but on every word that comes from the mouth of God."

Jesus was out on the desert, and the term 40 days was a commonly used expression in those times, denoting a lengthy period of time. It did not mean the exact time passed. This is a very important and simple message. Jesus understood without reading it in a book or online that the sustenance of a happy, nourished and sacred Life came from God within, and only from God.

The temptation Jesus experienced on the desert were the temptations in his thinking. He was no different than you or I. He had thoughts of doubt, thoughts of gaining worldly power and abundance. He had healed so many, in a worldly way, kingdoms would have been laid at his feet. Can't you just picture him thinking "I'm starving and could have 10 women, a warm bed, a belly full of food and here I am freezing and hungry." Those thoughts are the temptation of the serpent in all of us. Those thoughts could not care less about others and will step on another's neck in order to secure ourselves. He stuck it out, he knew his experience of the Garden of Eden was on the other side.

In the world we have so many false beliefs about God we are hesitant to turn ourselves all the way to Him. Religion has us all praying in a manner that can never be answered. God ONLY gives and gives abundantly, but the spirit of God cannot break through our worldly temptations and thoughts. The serpent within has us praying for things that would automatically come through His Grace, but for our phoning home throughout the day in prayer.

Prayer:

Father I am blessed in your eternal, gentle spirit and have been created in order to share the sacred. Amen.

Self- Awareness

Sometimes we avoid being self- aware; we don't want to experience the negative things we are thinking and feeling about ourselves. Whenever we are concerned with, or bothered by what someone else thinks about us, we are the ones who are not liking ourselves. If we keep our sights on those around us we are "safe" from the intense guilt, shame and dislike within. Stirring up drama about the people around us works like a charm to keep us unaware of our inner state.

Not moving about the world with an easy engaging smile, is to be moving about the world self-conscious, not self-aware. Self-consciousness has us caught up in thoughts of how we look in our clothes, how we sound when we speak.

I am feeling like going back to bed at this moment. It's St. Patty's and I have a head cold. Yup, I am normal weight and I feel fat and unattractive. I am feeling totally self-conscious. What can I do? Well first I want to recognize that I am feeling this way and I want to be nice to myself. I won't allow myself to get lost in feelings of self- pity or self- abasement. I do have enough self- awareness to know that if I am feeling good about me, nothing else matters. No one else's opinion adds, nor detracts, from how I feel about myself. THAT is always the truth no matter how I have, OR want to delude myself. NO ONE hurts anyone else's feelings.

You know what's funny? I usually sparkle and everyone talks to me. Not right now. I don't feel or look unfriendly, I am just not my normal, usual level of sparkle. What I notice when I am out and about around people is that they feel vulnerable. If they don't know you they wonder if you are going to be nice. What would it look like if everyone (including me) knew that no one's judgments adds, nor detracts from our value?

So back to feeling fat; riding along with that feeling for me would lead straight to food that would give me more of that experience. Therefore, I want to be aware today to do the opposite. I am checking in a lot about what to eat. When I am eating I am being careful not to numb my head cold, and to just go for inspired nourishment.

It's lunch time and I am surrounded by handsome dudes. Time to be self-aware and not listen to any thoughts in my head that might want to make me feel like crap. Why? Because when I am busy thinking like that I am not friendly, or easy going. I don't need anything from anyone. The world is sorely in need of a gentle Soul no matter what they look like. I really mean that. It doesn't matter what we look like, a gentle Soul is beautiful.

There is nothing more important than being self-aware. This also means being aware of what time of day you reach for how much, and what kind of foods? For me I am generally not hungry early in the day. Unless of course I am sick, feeling sorry for myself and wanting to eat the house. I like to sit in the middle of the day around 2 or 3 pm and eat as inspired. I may have a piece of fruit or an organic bar earlier, depending on how much activity and what I ate the night before. No automatic eating, EAT WHEN HUNGRY.

Eating any more than a snack at night leads right to weird dreams for me. That one simple change after becoming self- aware has made such a difference. If I slip into unconsciousness and eat too much I remind myself to remember next time. I deserve better than weird dreams and feeling lethargic in the morning.

If I find myself at a restaurant, or someone is cooking something awesome for me, it is no loss to pack it up for the middle of the next day! This is no hardship or even hard to do! I just need to remember! There are a bunch of holidays coming up and today is St. Patty's, I will keep these inspired thoughts in the forefront.

See? Self-awareness. How was I inspired when at peace? I can tell how I was inspired when at peace, this book is FULL of those inspirations. Take a look at what you eat and when. No need to decide to change a THING. Just observe and be aware, changes will come of themselves as you set your intentions with God. Inspiration is always shifting around and changing. Learn to trust your self - awareness.

When you are determined to become gentle with yourself and others you can FEEL something else trying to come forward. The ego's compulsive thoughts and opinions have been running the show and they are anything but gentle. When you become self aware and determined in one area of your life, you automatically begin to generalize the experience to all areas.

Do you want to be pinched, skinny and bitchy??? No, me neither. Lol. There are plenty of those around lovie; God's will for you and I is not that!

Self-awareness, how am I feeling about me right now? I feel a prayer coming on:

Prayer:

Thank you Father for creating me in your perfection. May I remember today to witness to the bread of Life flowing forth from my brother today. Your Will is the only true Will and it is my own. Thank you Father that your perfection guides me, but for my turning to you with empty hands. Amen

Nothing Has Gone Wrong

Allow this thought to permeate your very being because this is the absolute truth. Nothing has gone wrong carrying extra weight on the body. Unknowingly buffering ourselves from the Kingdom of Heaven is only a mistake. Now we know better and we observe.

All of the thoughts of self-hatred are the exact same thing as feeling excited about looking sexy. Can you absorb that? These bodies that we have are no different than any of our other worldly possessions. We take care of them and recognize that they are not *who* we are. The body is literally a communication device. We are demonstrating all of the time whether we believe these bodies are our identity, or not.

If we are bodily identified we will never be enough; I don't care who you are or what you do. This is vital for us to understand; no one in the world is completely comfortable all of the time in their "own" skin. We look at our history and it's not pretty. Some more than others, but I have yet to meet anyone honest who says they had an easy road in the world. Identifying in the world as a body would define you as experiencing a *rough* road.

I remember seeing someone advocating for black people and thinking "I wish the world would acknowledge the plight of single mothers." That opened a whole can of worms within myself that could never be closed or satisfied. Are you following me? If you want to carry a cross, you have one and I know it!

I am in NO WAY diminishing the plight of black people. What the carnal mind acted out with slavery is savage. That is EXACTLY what the carnal wants for me and you. ENSLAVEMENT. There is no evil man, woman or child; it's all that carnal mind that goes unchecked within the mind.

What is Soul identified? KNOWING that there is a reality above form and it is real and eternal. The body's eyes show us nothing, and the body's ears keep us deaf to the truth about us. In this place, above form, is where we meet without a body. We will never get to our sameness looking at each other's level of abundance, attractiveness, color of our skin, etc. We will never attain the everlasting peace of God and his comfort while just wanting all of that for ourselves alone. That is what slavery is, self-involvement.

Listening to the Voice for love in my mind around food has fast forwarded my trust and confidence in that Voice in all things. It makes no difference what the body's eyes are looking at, or what the ears are hearing, nothing has gone wrong. If we can allow that thought to permeate our mind when something has rocked our inner world, we are well on our way to being free.

As we allow our minds to seek out and practice true prayer, our lives begin to change. Some of us swift and drastic, some of us slow and steady. It all depends on our level of exposure to truth and our commitment to living it.

Prayer:

Thank you Father, I seek only your Will; for your Will is the only Will and therefore mine. I know you are the everlasting arms beneath all form. You are the force that seeks to love and care for your son. I am yours, I am grateful to you O Father. I am blessed by you through my brothers and they are blessed by you through me. You are my only want, my only need, my bread of life, thank you Father. Amen.
Glorify God

God is the only power in this world. There is another false shadow called the carnal mind that dies of neglect, without our feeding it. It's thoughts and actions have been running the world since the Garden of Eden and eating from the tree of good and evil. It is the story of the Son of God moving from the experience of perfection to the experience of good and evil by giving into temptation. Does it sound familiar?

It is our belief in good and evil that sustains it. There's nothing we can do to overcome the belief in good and evil. The only answer is to rise completely up above it, in our minds, to perfection where it simply does not exist. Jesus refers to this state of mind in *A Course In Miracles* as ***"above the battle ground."***

I like to do substitute teaching. I love the collaboration, the kids and everything about it. I remember being startled at how easy it was to know the parents simply by knowing the children. Kids are so much like their environment. Unless you are a teacher, you have no idea how transparent one's parenting is. Seriously, it's like there's no separation between parent and kid.

Who am I representing as I walk in the world? Whose voice am I reflecting? What am I choosing to talk about? Where do my interests lay? Is my mind locked into condemnation and suffering, or am I committed to innocence? *"Let he who is without sin cast the first stone"* comes to mind.

There is an invisible force that is emitting light in the very center of our being. I have seen it, it looks just like the halo around Jesus in the Da Vinci painting of the Last Supper. There is a glow inside and around each of us. At times I have seen this halo around people and sometimes I can see it glow around their entire bodies.

We have a parent and that parent is God. When we listen and are inspired by the Voice for Love within us, we function in a certain way in the world. We become more gentle with others and begin to see our unforgiveness and drop it like a rock. We understand that unforgiveness is a tether to the world and that it is not our Father's will. All of our unforgiveness and self- destruction with food is centered around believing we are a separate "i" from God.

I don't want to make myself guilty and try to invoke the ego to act in some puritanical "Godly" way. Oh no, that would be missing the whole point. As I allow my mind to dwell more frequently with these thoughts of truth, I feel better and want more. As I listen within, it becomes more and more apparent to those at hand.

God's Will is the end of all suffering. God knows not of suffering and listening to the Voice for love would never ever lead us to suffering of any kind. We don't need to step on anyone to get ahead, or to get "ours". There is an infinite amount of abundance in God to go around.

Communing with God on a regular basis shows. Similarly, not communing with God regularly shows big time too. It's just like with the little kids at school, you can see who is being loved and who is barely acknowledged. We are just like those little kids. God our Father would have us know him and glorify him because it is the natural, happy function of his children.

Prayer:

Thank you Father for in you I am made whole. There is no other Will but yours and your Will is my own. In you I am filled with the grace of your perfection and purity. Your everlasting arms beneath all form hold me in your loving, caring, sweet embrace. I am in the Garden of Eden, beyond good and evil with you. You created this beautiful garden just for me, I stand here on sacred ground with you. I have no function beyond glorifying you and your magnificence. I want no other function than the happiness of glorifying you. Thank you Father, thank you Father, thank you Father. Amen.

Our happy function is to glorify God, to glorify our only true parent and Father. We don't need to offer ourselves some kind of concept about what that is, we need only pause and listen within ourselves. This listening increases and becomes more natural with our remembering, desire and practice. God's voice and direction are right within us but for our turning within through contemplation, prayer and meditation.

When we think of God and his purity, we are visiting our parent. When we consider the perfection of the Garden of Eden above the belief in good and evil we are visiting our parent. When we sit at a red light, relax our bodies and remember the glowing light within us, we are remembering our parent.

When we meditate we are visiting our parent. We are relaxing into the everlasting arms beneath all form we are with our Creator. We can do this for a minute or for hours, there is no set way in which to commune with yours and my Father.

When we pray we are thanking and adoring our Father, we are recounting His gifts to us and being thankful. PRAYER IS NOTHING ELSE. We praise, adore and thank with empty hands. *"Seek ye first the Kingdom and all things will be added."*

God is glorified in our happiness, vitality, easy humor, abundance and radiant health. God is glorified in our honesty, integrity and in our gentle relationships at hand. God is glorified in our listening to and being inspired by Him. It is vital to not limit God by our asking for or even being grateful for specifics. Our thoughts about specifics block the God Vibe.

The Body's Eyes

The body's eyes are showing us nothing. We are
taught in spiritual doctrine that they were created in
order to keep us hypnotized by what they are seeing.
In the world they are seeing differences and division
of every sort of good and evil.

Here is an important question for me to ask myself.
Why do I want to lose weight, or be more slim? I may
be looking in the mirror and seeing fat there and
telling myself I want less of it. Now I am feeling
emotion and am locked into what the body's eyes are
showing me. This is the ultimate in separation,
picking out specifics with the body's eyes and
wanting to make change. God's grace is in
everything. If we are able to be completely honest
with ourselves, we can see that everything is at least
a little off kilter when we are carrying extra
weight. Good news is that when we regularly
commune with God, all things are set right. God is
the real cause of all things and all things in form
effects. Did that land? Change happens in the mind,
not in rearranging form. When change is of God, it
effects all levels, all things.

Every experience has it's beginning in thought. Every single thing that we are looking at right now had its beginning in thought. The mind is very powerful and we are taught in scripture that Adam and Eve were in the Garden of Eden in perfection. The Garden of Eden is a state of mind where the only cause is God and therefore all things perfection.

The story of Genesis is a pretty wild ride. The only way it makes sense and is in alignment with the *New Testament* and *A Course in Miracles* is like this….

Adam and Eve were told by God not to eat from the tree of good and evil (duality). AFTER they ate from the tree a punishing God came into the Garden of Eden. THAT WAS NOT GOD. It was the ego/serpent appearing as God. This was all happening at the level of MIND.

We have made a punishing God of Him ever since. The ego/serpent was able to convince them (humans appearing as Adam and Eve) to feel deep shame and to throw THEMSELVES out of the garden.

Any true modern day mystic is trying to find their way back to our original state of mind with God in innocence and perfection. This is happening through the forgiveness of the BELIEF, see that??? THE BELIEF in good and evil.

God would never ever ever ever cast His Beloved Son from Heaven. It was a trick of mind!

So back to the mirror. We are being deceived by a power that is not real. It is powerful only by our belief in it. Look in the mirror KNOWING that you are surrounded literally by the light of perfection.

As we move more into true prayers throughout the day, God will be guiding our actions and the miraculous will literally begin to appear before our eyes. To no longer shame, punish or make guilty, within OR without, is to become enlightened.

Prayer:

Thank you Father for your perfect love surrounds me and all things seen and unseen. I look to you and your Will of happiness, freedom and perfection. Your Will is only good, your will is light. Your Will is mine. Amen.

Impersonalize The Ego/Serpent

Just as we are one and the same in the spirit and mind of God, the ego-serpent is one thing as well. It appears as many scary-ass things, but it is all the same. It is all FALSE. We get to the experience of innocence by seeing it as one big-ass major hypnotism appearing as a lot of things. They all fall under the umbrella of sin, sickness and death. Anything other than perfect happiness is a form of sickness; finances, turbulent relationships, the whole shebang a form of sickness that is not personal. Everyone in the world is under ONE SPELL of the carnal mind, appearing as many.

You may look in the mirror and not like the size of your big ole butt, and someone else may have an on-going beef with the next door neighbor; it's all coming from the same place and it's all impersonal. Are you seeing that? Anything other than perfection and perfect happiness is a part of the grand illusion. This is the ultimate form of forgiveness.

Rejection

Adam and Eve is the story of creation. They were in the Garden of Eden where it was perfection. This was Heaven where there was only happiness, abundance, communion and joy. As the story goes, God told Eve not to eat from the tree of good and evil and she did. Not only did she, she got Adam to do it too. Along came angry God and booted them out of the garden (Heaven). The "god" was the serpent disguised as God. It was only Adam and Eve's belief in it that gave it any power over them.

Adam and Eve became filled with shame and self-consciousness and were cast out from a (false) wrathful God, only to face a life of suffering (good and evil).

This is the story of the ego entering into the mind of the Son of God, and lifting numerous false gods. We have literally swallowed its beliefs in guilt and shame and an unenlightened mind (which is all of us) is replaying this false drama over and over.

This is no light and breezy thing to realize. This is major heavy-duty stuff and may make you a little light-headed while you contemplate it. I have experienced some intense anxiety in the realization. This is THE first experience of deception.

Any time you have experienced rejection in this world it was the impersonal nature of the serpent and 100% not real. There IS no rejection in God. When you have felt shame about being fat, when you were passed over for that job, when you were blown off by that love interest. Guess what? All a re-enactment of that FIRST false experience. YOU are not good enough GET OUT. Or the flip side of not wanting to experience rejection, we then project upon others. See the cycle? We are either in the emotional pain body of being rejected from heaven, OR we are not wanting to feel ourselves as rejected. SO, we then reject others.

Now reading these words, or writing these words is not enough. I have sat in my mind and reviewed every painful belief in rejection I have held there. We all have such scripts, they run deep by design. Do not be afraid to look your deepest feelings of rejection and the people attached to it right in the eye. I am here to tell you that it is not real. I wrote a whole entire book about the mind burning experience of the Dark Night Of The Soul. It's all in there, where this original darkness can take you. We are all cloaked in darkness and this IS the way out. The belief in rejection, and therefore guilt and punishment runs deep.

Have you ever eaten when feeling rejected? Have you ever eaten when you felt like a complete hollowed-out loser? Have you ever eaten because you feel alone? Like one might feel had they been cast from Eden? It would be funny were it not for all of the pain and suffering it has caused. NO ONE WAS CAST OUT OF EDEN/HEAVEN.

When I was pregnant and divorcing I had regular appointments at the hospital in Boston. I would literally laugh and tell my friend I had an appointment at the Bakery on the first floor. I was burying my resonance in God with food. God was the only cure for my broken heart, and I was making it worse by distancing myself from my Father! Ugh.

Remember this; no one can reject you. Only you can reject yourself. Once you really take this truth into your mind, you will never be offended by what anyone ever says to you again. You will see anything that appears less than loving, for the dark spell that it is. Jesus broke that spell. We are too.

Each time we feel inside of ourselves that someone else is trying to diminish us, we are reliving the false experience given by the serpent in the Garden of Eden. We will never be free as long as we are hypnotized in the wanting anyone to act any differently. As we go to God in True Prayer, we are strengthened in our relationship with God, our true Father.

Prayer:

Thank you Father for your love for me, which you have placed within me. Your grace goes before me in all things that are whole, perfect and filled with your light. The only truth about me is your wholeness and perfection. I trust in you Father that your Will is the ONLY Will and there is nothing else but you and your love for me that is true and eternal. In you Father I am fully accepted and adored. You know only of my perfection as you have created me in your image of perfection. I am with you, and you with me. I am in you and you are in me. Thank you Father for the truth of who I am in you. I am grace, I am your grace, for now, for always, throughout eternity. Amen.

Security

Who isn't seeking the experience of some kind of
security in the world? I believe it is Louis Hay who
suggested an affirmation of feeling secure for weight
loss. No one in this world feels secure. How could
that be? I don't know anyone who does not walk
around with feelings of insecurity with varying
degrees.

Ironically, we reach for extra food for that feeling of
inner security, and it gives us the exact opposite
experience. There is no reason to feel weird about
this. If you take a look at every single thing that
anyone reaches to for feelings of security, it fails
them sooner or later.

People who are emotionally invested in their money,
looks, lover, prestige, home, kids are ALL afraid of
losing them. Notice I said "invested," these things of
themselves are neutral. It's built into the system of
failure that is the world. Everyone feels like we are
going to arrive just around the next bend.

Just like looking for relief from eating an entire cake.
Or when we are relieved to know that GREAT
looking person wants us! Then what? We all know

eating the cake for the sake of relief makes us feel WORSE. We all have seen people, and heard the music of those of us undone by romantic love, gone terribly wrong.

You know why all of these things fail us? They are false gods that we are turning to for relief instead of to the real deal...GOD.

When we decide the cake will make us feel better we have cause and effect all turned around. We are looking for the cake to be of good, of relief, we WANT to feel love and security! No? Of course we do! Who doesn't? It's the motivator for all of the hideous, backwards behavior in the world. Seeking security where it CAN'T be found at anyone's expense!

If the feelings can't be found in one cookie, how about 12? If I can't feel secure with one woman, how about 2 or 3? Are you following me here? Can you see it in your own life?

I remember learning in my first book that I would never be thin as long as I was seeking it for myself alone. It's like having 10 cupcakes and 5 boyfriends. There will never be enough *things* to create feelings of lasting security. There is no security in wanting anything for myself alone. When our vibe is high, we are meant to shine that light everywhere without limit, or prejudice, that is what keeps the vibe going.

We are like the petal of a flower cut off from it's source and that source is God. We are unknowingly seeking God in all of these things. It is such a simple thing to get connected back the sunlight (light) of God. I am not sure how prayer took such a wrong turn, but the way we are praying in the world is not serving us by leading us back to our true security.

Does it mean that through seeking God's Will we cannot have any of these things? Absolutely not! When we commune with God we unblock the thoughts of imperfection in our own minds and things are delivered to us washed clean with His Love.

When we go to God and experience communion with Him, there is nothing that compares to that. This communion cannot be taken away in any circumstances, it is eternal. My whole entire life I thought that the Will of God MUST be the most boring and uninteresting thing on planet Earth. Why did I think that? Because of what the the world and religion has made of prayer. We don't need to pray to God for forgiveness because God does not condemn us! See how that thought comes from the false experience in the Garden of Eden? We all know that praying for things does not work!

I remember being on my knees in desperation and praying to Jesus. I was so pissed off because I had been so devoted. I wanted relief from the experience of sorrow that I was feeling. I clearly heard the still, small voice telling me that I was seeking for the "sins of Lee" to be forgiven and that they and she did not exist. Not in an earthly no parents, sinful, neglected and abused way. The world is abusive! Guess what? You are not of the world. You are spirit and have a parent in spirit.

Security is found in true prayer. This is where we commune as we are in spirit with our Father, in spirit which is God. When the blocks to happiness and security are removed from our mind, his love and gifts come to us. We are blocking the very thing that we seek with our own ideas. Does this happen by default in the world? Absolutely! All of the time this happens. Have you ever completely given up on something and let it go? Then the answer just comes to you? Ever exclaim "I give up" then the situation turns around? Of course you have, we all have!

Often times things work out way better than we were hoping for in the letting go.

Prayer:

Thank you Father for the truth that is you. In you I am made complete. Your treasure of love and security surround me with infinite care and goodness. You have set up a treasure house of your gifts for your Son who is me in your Kingdom. Thank you Father, thank you Father, your Will is my one Will joined with yours.

Impersonalize Darkness

I want to allow my mind to go wide with this thought and really take it in. There is total freedom in not taking darkness personally. Personal is what someone says to you about the fat on your hips, sickness, fighting, terrorism and on and on.

What if you really saw that darkness has an impersonal nature just as love does? Darkness is floating around and always looking for a place to land where it is made welcome. Yes, when someone is screaming and yelling at you they are under a dark spell. Yes, when you are looking at the fat on your hips and bumming out, again, a spell. You can throw all of your thoughts about your hips right in the trash can, pray truly, eat by the four principles and leave it up to God and his perfection.

Darkness is all one thing, it wants us unhappy so that it can grow. When we ignore and do not utilize its thoughts, it literally disappears.

You and I are responsible for seeing the darkness in our own minds and tossing it right into the trash and not utilizing it. We are taught in *A Course In Miracles,* and by Jesus in the *New Testament*, not to believe what the body's eyes are showing us. Why is that? Because they are always showing us differences and tragedy.

I have seen many times halos around people's heads and around objects, trees and such. There is literally light emanating from every living thing. This light wants to flow freely and go before us in all things. Our thoughts block it.

My grandfather, John Patrick Mullally, was the most loving man I have ever known. He read his Bible and was very devoted to his fellow man. He passed on when I was 30 years old and came to me in a dream. I asked him if he still believed in Catholicism on the other side. He picked a leaf off of a tree and light flowed out of the leaf. He told me he believed in all things of God-nature, all good things.

If God goes before you in the super market, at church, in a board meeting, on a date, at a school conference, in the pantry, God makes all things right. What that means is to forgive (look beyond) our ideas about everything and KNOW God is with us.

There is a term in the world called "free will." There is no will other than God's. Any other will is nothing but a feverish nightmare and if you look at all of the decisions you have made by yourself you will see that this is true.

We hear frightening things every day with the body's ears and see scary-ass things with the body's eyes as well.

"What makes this world seem real except your own denial of the truth which lies beyond? What but your thoughts of misery and death obscure the perfect happiness and the Eternal Life your Father wills for you? And what could hide what cannot be concealed except illusion? What could keep from you what you already have except your choice to see it not, denying it is there?" A Course In Miracles

I get frightened by the same things as everyone else does. When I read this above passage it is amazing to me that Jesus does not want me believing, or acknowledging MOST of what I hear.
Depersonalizing darkness is an active activity of the mind.

I remember my daughter came and sat on my bed and was feeling upset. I knew in my mind the moment she opened her mouth I was not going to believe in a word she said. In God it is only good news. My daughter was completely open and ready for a shift out of darkness, that made it like magic. I looked at her face fraught with anxiety and met it with a big smile. She said " I hope I can smile after I tell you what I need to say."

I literally felt every word coming from her mouth met with the light of happiness; it didn't even matter what she was saying. I heard words come from my mouth that were unlocking the keys to the false chains upon her mind. She started smiling too, and before you knew it we were sitting there grinning at each other. I am getting tears in my eyes right now picturing the innocence of the moment and her sweet face relaxing.

Was it me??? ABSOLUTELY not. I was able to have faith in God to be with us and set the matter straight. It had nothing to do with me. She offered me her bread of life in her willingness to reach for it; and we both received from the Father. We all share one Father who is everywhere waiting to care for us. We need to call on him and deny the denial of truth, which IS the fear thoughts in our own minds. We have to give ourselves PERMISSION to believe in Jesus and His word because it is God's.

4 Jesus answered, "It is written: 'Man shall not live on bread alone, but on every word that comes from the mouth of God." Matthew 4:4

We offer one another the bread of life through our words that are inspired by God. Every word we speak depicts what we are believing in; either the ONE WILL or the false, thin, black veil of untruth. We are enormously powerful in God we are told. The solution from every malady that the world has ever faced is forgiveness. We are told to deny the denial of truth. Impersonalize darkness because it is not so and it makes it easier to look beyond.

The scariest thing you hear today will lose it's hold on you if you do ONE thing. Impersonalize it, see it as the great deception, allow yourself to *(not)* go there.

Prayer:

Thank you Father for your one Will for it is all that I desire. I am made whole in you and I rest in your everlasting arms beneath all form. Thank you Father for your Grace, Abundance, and Perfection. In you Father are all things set right. In you I am raised in light as was my brother Lazarus. Thank you Father for your release from the tomb into the light. Amen.

Perfection

We have no idea what perfection is. Here in the world at the mercy of the ego-serpent mind we are always at its mercy. The mind that runs the world is fraught with doubt; it interrupts our creativity and inspiration constantly.

There have been some that have been able to see halo's around the heads of others. Artists have portrayed it, the museums are filled with such depictions. I have also seen these halos. These halos are the light and love of God that is within each and every one of us. The more connected we are to God, the more our halo can shine, the more our light shines.

When we hear stories about God not favoring, we attach human qualities to God. God does not favor because there is nowhere that God is not. That light does not shine more, or less intensely in, or around anyone. However, it is our awareness of, and belief in something else no matter how false, that keeps us from the power of the light.

Think back to the Garden of Eden. Consider what total perfection might be. There was only the mind and love of God in the Garden of Eden. Perfection would mean that nothing died, aged or withered. There was only continuous abundance and radiant well-being and health.

Perfection would be complete gentleness and understanding between all living things in the Garden. Pondering perfection and remembering that this is the true Will, and the only Will of God, is vital to our awakening. When we spend a lot of time pondering perfection, the intrusions of the world loosen their effect. When we hear of something catastrophic our minds can go to our Vision and Truth in the Garden of Eden with God. The Garden of Eden IS Heaven on Earth and it is God's Will for us.

Pray perfection in order to bring it more fully into our minds. Pray perfection often.

Prayer:

Thank you Father for shining your perfection in and around your Son which I am. I live, love and abide in your one Will. Your Will for your Son is perfection, radiance, truth and abundance beyond measure. Thank you Father for your perfect love, thank you Father for perfection and nothing else will ever be your Will. There is only one Will and that is your Will.
Perfection lights the way, perfection fills me, perfection is the truth, perfection is the treasure of heaven. Amen.

One Will

The term "one Will" has been misrepresented by religion and spiritual leaders since time began. I had the one Will of God confused with what religion has made of God, so why on earth would I reach out to that?

What is the one Will of God? The one Will of God is the creative force behind all things that are perfect, kind and good. It's true and when you learn to pray truly and practice it, you will not need anyone to tell you of it.

I used to think that I was the most hip and happening thing and that God's Will, just the term, was beyond BORING. When I look deeply into my mind for the answer to why this is I can see it is misrepresentation that brought me to that idea.

What if we understood beyond a shadow of a doubt what God's Will was? What if we understood with every fiber of our being that there is a God who gently blankets all things with perfection? This is no small thing and I have had tears in my eyes three times writing this passage. Nothing has gone wrong, we have always been safe and protected from all that ails us in God. The ONLY time we have EVER suffered has been at our own hand.

You may be wondering how this ties into food. Am I doing some kind of tricky bait and switch? Absolutely not. Whatever cross it is that we are carrying in this world, we have given it to ourselves. If you have read my first book you would know that this is a very drastic thing for me to be saying. I am saying it because it is the truth.

If God's Will is perfection, and I assure you that it is, what would I look like? Feel like? Sound like? If I were practicing true prayer, forgiveness? Forgiveness being defined as looking beyond the world. Who knows right? I mean I have no clue and that is an awesome place to be. Trust me, I have never brought perfection to my own doorstep. This I do know, true prayer and forgiveness sets ALL things right. To not know how to eat, speak, walk, exercise, sing, etc, brings us into a place of receptivity. When we believe that all that is given is good and filled with Grace, we are humbled and ready to receive.

When we clear our minds of all of our ideas, we begin to experience the miraculous (perfection) of God. We approach food with EMPTY minds and

ASK. Then we go to God ... *Thank you God. You fortify me, you nourish me, I am blessed in you! Thank you Father. Amen.* In this type of prayer you will KNOW how to eat, you will love what you eat, your eating will become sacred because it is and you are. Eat your gluten free, organic cupcake, or whatever it is you are inspired to eat in God!

If you get a tummy ache from eating wheat, don't eat it! I am happier than I have ever been in my entire life, and I take two iron pills for anemia every morning. Will I always? No. Do I for now? Yes. God has me on the "til further notice" plan.

We don't need to put any carts before any horses and start doing things that cause us anxiety. That could never be God's Will. As we move into our reality of perfect worthiness, things shift and change around of themselves through God. NEVER tell yourself "I should be able to do this," or "I should be this way or that." Why? Because that is the assertion of your own will again, and we all know where that has gotten us.

It says in the Bible that our way will be made straight in God. We have caused our own suffering and in our letting go it is automatically made straight. God is not assertive; we are blocking his will. We are so sure that we know stuff and it is good and great news that we don't know anything. The even better news is that perfection itself is flowing to us but for our welcome.

As you move more into your experience of the Will of God, be sure to remember where your Grace is coming from. Don't cut of the supply by taking any personal credit for anything. All glory goes to God and that is a good and great thing.

Prayer:

Thank you Father for in you I am made whole in ways beyond my wildest imagination. You are the power that sets all things right. You bring me forward and nourish me in your Garden of Eden. I am blessed by you and in you. You God are the I, you are in me and I in you. Your bread of life is all I seek and in you I am so grateful. Amen.

April 1, 2016

Kelly noticed Lee was signed into google docs at the same time and started to write to Lee:

Kelly: Hi mom!

Lee: Haha hi kel! Lol
I loved your Instagram so much today thank you God thru Kelly!
I just did a video...shit is going down Kel!

Kelly: Having so much fun with my kids today (talking about her High School students). Having students teach for April Fools' Day.

Lee: Awesome! That sounds like an inspired idea!

Kelly: They are fun and it is so easy to feel God's love through them.
Hahahahaha!!!

Mom I learned a HARD background for one of my students today, and I got back to my desk and did some true prayer. Then she was in class and I had her play and teach. I could see she was feeling God's love.

Lee: WOW! You are speaking the truth!!!!
I am telling you this true prayer stuff is tough on the veggie mascara!
Second time already in this message I have tears in my eyes...oye. Lol

YES! This IS the mechanism of healing!
Everyone who touches your awareness will heal as
you pray. Who is healing them??? GOD!!!!

Kelly: GOD IS baby
I feel this strange mixture of peace and seeing light
and anxiety/ terror in my gut.

Lee: I am going to do it (true prayer) right now.

Prayer:
Thank you Father for your ONE WILL for in it
there is ONLY perfection!!! I am blessed by you
and there is nothing but your love for me in the
Garden of Eden. I would be here with you right
now and through eternity. You are the Father and
you are my one Source of light and all things
blessed, good and sacred. Thank you Father for
in you I have been made whole and
complete. Amen.

Kelly: This just started playing in my mind
(Woodstock by Crosby Stills and Nash)

"Got to get ourselves back to the Garden....
Got to get back to the land and set my soul free"

Lee: OMGod making me cry again!
I am so grateful, filled with grace.
There is nothing to fear and when that begins to
dawn you will be crying all of the time. Like "holy
crap, there is nothing to fear. I am REALLY not on
my own."
I am going to write now and food shop sweet heart.

Kelly: It amazing that something (anxiety) that feels
so real is such a deception

Okay love you mamma have a perfect day xoxoxo

Woodstock

Crosby, Stills & Nash

Well, I came upon a child of God
He was walking along the road
And I asked him, Tell where are you going?
This he told me
Said, I'm going down to Yasgur's Farm,
Gonna join in a rock and roll band.
Got to get back to the land and set my soul free.
We are stardust, we are golden,
We are billion year old carbon,
And we got to get ourselves back to the garden.
Well, then can I walk beside you?
I have come to lose the smog,

114

And I feel like I'm a cog in something turning.
And maybe it's the time of year,
Yes and maybe it's the time of man.
And I don't know who I am,
But life is for learning.
We are stardust, we are golden,
We are billion year old carbon,
And we got to get ourselves back to the garden.
We are stardust, we are golden,
We are billion year old carbon,
And we got to get ourselves back to the garden.
By the time we got to Woodstock,
We were half a million strong
And everywhere was a song and a celebration.
And I dreamed I saw the bomber death planes
Riding shotgun in the sky,
Turning into butterflies
Above our nation.
We are stardust, we are golden,
We caught in the devil's bargain,
And we got to get ourselves back to the garden

Awareness

This world and everything in it is a big fat lie. There is nothing you can point to here that contains the perfection of the Garden of Eden, which is the metaphor for heaven. Not with the body's eyes you can't. There is another sense in the area of the third eye located mid-forehead. This is where the perception of perfection is perceived. This is the porthole for Vision.

God is beneath all form, there is nowhere that God is not. The only thing that is blocking our awareness is our thoughts and ideas that we place before God. We believe in the myth of the Garden of Eden and being thrown out of heaven, and we are always re-enacting the impossible. Only our thinking makes it so.

Anything that is right and gentle in this world is inspired by God. The inspiration is unseen, and the good and kindness are God's fruit.

When we begin to deny the denial of truth in all of its forms, miracles start to go down. We MUST remember that it is all God and to take any personal credit for any of it is error of large magnitude. To cut

God out of the picture is to limit our fruitage from the Father.

Do you believe that most of what you see and hear in the world is not true? Perfection is of spirit and in this perfection all form is set right. What is the secret to all of this? True prayer and union with God. There is nothing else to achieve.

The Master Jesus taught that we are as branches cut off from tree and withering.

John 15 - Jesus The True Vine

"1 I am the true vine, and My Father is the keeper of the vineyard. 2 He cuts off every branch in Me that bears no fruit, and every branch that does bear fruit, He prunes to make it even more fruitful. 3 You are already clean because of the word I have spoken to you. 4 Remain in Me, and I will remain in you. Just as no branch can bear fruit by itself unless it remains in the vine, neither can you bear fruit unless you remain in Me.
5 I am the vine and you are the branches. The one who remains in Me, and I in him, will bear much fruit. For apart from Me you can do nothing. 6 If anyone does not remain in Me, he is

like a branch that is thrown away and withers. Such branches are gathered up, thrown into the fire, and burned. 7 If you remain in Me and My words remain in you, ask whatever you wish, and it will be done for you. 8 This is to My Father's glory, that you bear much fruit, proving yourselves to be My disciples.

No Greater Love

9 As the Father has loved Me, so have I loved you. Remain in My love. 10 If you keep My commandments, you will remain in My love, just as I have kept My Father's commandments and remain in His love. 11 I have told you these things so that My joy may be in you and your joy may be complete.

12 This is My commandment, that you love one another as I loved you. 13 Greater love has no one than this, that he lay down his life for his friends.

14 You are My friends if you do what I command you. 15 No longer do I call you servants, for a servant does not understand what his master is doing. But I have called you friends, because everything I have learned from My Father I have made known to you. 16 You did not choose Me, but I chose you. And I appointed you to go and bear fruit—fruit that will remain—so that whatever you ask the Father in My name, He will give you. 17 This is My command to you: Love one another."

When you perceive any imperfection of yourself, or another DROP IT LIKE IT'S HOT from your mind. Heaven will come to Earth through your awareness of ONLY heaven. Who else do you suppose is going to usher it in?

Is food the last temptation for you? If you are reading this book it may be. How awesome is that? What a simple way to lift one's awareness heavenward by noticing our Earth-bound thoughts around food. When I am listening around food I am AWARE. The awareness of what I do around food is awakening me to awareness around everything. Not listening the Voice for Love in my mind around food leads me to a lowered vibration. I can see clearly how I feel cut-off from God's Grace when I over-feed the body. Is God blowing me off? Absolutely not, I pulled the shade, not God. That's okay, I can lift the shade right up, so long as I am AWARE of what I am doing.

If I am not listening to God when speaking with the people in my life I feel disconnected as well. I listen to God, everything goes smoothly. I start believing in the hypnotism of the world? BOOM lowered vibration again. God is a high vibration and we must lift UP. God can not lower God's vibration and that is a good and great thing.

Prayer:

Thank you Father for your perfection and your guidance in all things. I would turn to you in all things. Thank you Father for in you I am blessed immeasurably. Amen

Lust (for food)

Lust is defined as an overwhelming desire, or craving. Have you ever lusted after another human being? We are filled with our desires. Lust for food is the same. The carnal mind is filled with the lust and cravings for its own satisfaction. Up above its level of thought there are no cravings or desires. This does not mean we do not thoroughly enjoy food, sex, nice weather, things, etc. Oh no, once all of these things are no longer reached for to fill some sort of lack, we enjoy them all the more. We enjoy them more thoroughly because we no longer look to them for our happiness and or satisfaction. We have touched the God-Vibe and no longer look without ourselves for relief where it cannot be found. This IS the ego/carnal minds credo:

"Seek and do not find." A Course In Miracles

The seeking and not finding relief keeps us stuck in the circular madness of not finding relief within a (carnal) thought system that will NEVER deliver.

When food is no longer lusted for, it takes on another purpose. Just as in sex, when it is done as a practice of union and tenderness, it only adds to our feelings

121

of connectedness with God. Can we view food in the same way? Absolutely!

We all know the road of lust; it initially appears to feed something within us. On the way into the iced cupcakes, or hard abs, it all looks good. That is until we don't fit into our jeans any longer, or our man is in bed with our best friend. I insist that the cupcake take me to nirvana. I insist that the hard male body will do the job, when ONLY the God-Vibe (above thought) brings lasting happiness. We are here in the world and finding our way back to the Garden of Eden in our minds. Would God wish to take food and sex away from us? No, so long as we bring the purity of God into everything, it will be washed clean of all pain and suffering. Without God we have, and can only bring, pain and suffering to our doorstep.

Are you getting this? This is the ultimate pattern that is the metaphor of parenting in the world. Let's bring God into it. We want to feed our kids right. We want them to eat when hungry and be nourished. We want to feed their TRUE hunger, not their cravings. What is their true hunger? God. Can God be reached through our lustful impulses? No way.

This reminds me of listening to God within me while raising teenage girls. I told them I wanted them to wait to have sex, until they could feel comfy, smiling and laughing, while eating leftover Chinese in the sheets with their lover. This paints a picture of innocence and the Garden of Eden. God in me was teaching them to mature spiritually, and to avoid the pitfalls of lust.

Lust is the serpent, and we can't change that anymore than we can change the Love of God. We don't need to tear any band aids off and scare ourselves. True Prayer is the solvent and awareness keeps us on track . Awareness also bumps us back on track when we fall off.

The good news is that God is here, there, everywhere, including within me and you. We lift up in True Prayer, we enter into God's Kingdom. This sort of prayer lifts our vibration heavenward.

Prayer:

Thank you Father for within me is your light. You guide me here in all things and all I need is to turn to you. Your perfection covers over all ideas and inspiration. You are magnificent and I am yours. Your light within guides my way and I am blessed by you every moment of every day. I would reach for your Will, in your Will is heaven and all things good. In your Will is perfection beyond my wildest imaginings. Thank you Father. Thank you Father. Thank you Father. Amen.

Appetites - Illusion

Appetites are all of the body. When we believe we are a limited body and nothing else, our appetites have us. However, there is a much bigger part of us, much more than the body that has no appetites. It's content, abundant and happy and literally has no needs, or desires.

In the larger part of us, up above the world and the appetites of the body, is our freedom. You and I are spirit dwelling in the Garden of Eden right now. The Garden of Eden is the world of perfection, otherwise known as heaven where God is and nothing else.

Each time we entertain words of truth within the mind, we are taking a step back closer to the Garden of Eden. Up above all thoughts of the world; in quiet this resides within. We need not even fully reach the state of heaven, a tiny grain of sand is enough to transform our entire inner experience of ourselves and the world around us.

When we want to overfeed the body it is clear to see this appetite at work. What is it that wants to use food for soothing? Take it back a step further? Why do we need soothing in the first place? Living a life from a perspective of the body is so limited and lacking, it can only lead to appetites seeking relief. That is all that is going on with appetites, the seeking of relief from limitation. Limitation is painful.

When we leave our appetites and desires behind and enter into True Prayer we are approaching communion on a level that is very satisfying. We ask nothing specific and receive more than our limited mind can give us.

When we take that first step to sooth through a bodily appetite, we then begin a chain of events that become more difficult to back out of with each step. The first cookie did not do the trick, so maybe two, or ten? Then we begin to feel foggy, and are not as alert and available to those around us.

Now we are so far away from any real comfort, which is communion, that we are just lost. We literally find ourselves in one another. With every encounter with another Soul contains deep satisfaction. It is the complete opposite of bodily appetite.

So how do we get there? By remembering. I am literally moving away from communion with my fellows by choosing bodily appetites. There is the clear, beautiful perception of the Soul (The Christ which is you), and there are bodily appetites. It IS one or the other.

When we are perceiving the innocence, perfection and beauty of another, we are simultaneously perceiving it in ourselves. Whatever we see "there" we are feeling here. We cut ourselves off from our divinity without, we cannot feel it within.

There is self- satisfaction that is of the body and there is Self -satisfaction that is real and for everyone. The first one leads to every type of sorrow, and the second leads to peace and a beautiful experience of life.

What if bodily appetites were created in order to keep us unaware of our divinity within? What if it's that simple? As we perfect and get more used to our God- vibe the rest just falls away along with all of its appetites for destruction.   Every sad song ever written, every illness, every image of poverty and lack, every form of abuse that you can conjure has come from these appetites. We become oblivious to the dictates of error when we forget. By immersing in the truth through True Prayer, we remember more and more.

Prayer:

Thank you Father for in you I have been made whole with no needs of any kind. I would not place a will before your perfect and abundant Will. Thank you Father for I would dwell with you in the abundant Garden of Eden where there is no hunger of any kind. I see your perfection in all things, and I would not raise a false god before you. Thank you father for your precious Souls that are all about me. In them I perceive your Garden all day long. When I am on my own, I remember them and your perfection all hours of the night. You have blessed me eternally and it is your beautiful Will in which I trust and you are my only desire. You are my first desire; you are my last. Amen.

The Body - Will

To think that there are two wills is a great error of mind. There is only the Will of the Father, and any other will is a nightmare. Anything that any Soul attempts according to a foreign will, always leads to inner disaster. There is the will of flesh which is not real, and there is the one Will of God. This cannot be contemplated, emphasized and meditated upon enough.

There is a passage in the Essene Gospel of Peace that describes the false will perfectly. The false will is referred to as ego, Satan, Beelzebub.

"For no man can serve two masters. For either he serves Beelzebub and his devils or else he serves our Earthly Mother and her angels. Either he serves death or he serves life. I tell you truly, happy are those that do the laws of life and wander not upon the paths of death. For in them the forces of life wax strong and they escape the plagues of death." Essene Gospel Of Peace - Book One

"Happy are you, that you would cast off the power of Satan, for I will lead you into the kingdom of our Mother's angels, where the power of Satan cannot enter." Essene Gospel Of Peace - Book One

The term "masters" is in reference to following two wills. Casting off the power of Satan means to reject the thoughts of the false will in the mind. The only way to achieve this is to keep the thoughts of the Will of God active in the mind through true prayer. True prayer is affirmation of truth in thought that leads to receptive mode and communion with God.

The Will of the Father is an internal experience. When we practice stillness, His Will comes forward in our experience. To follow the false will, entails the experience of anxiety. When we are relaxed and resting in the Will of God we are at peace. When peace begins to slip away we know that we are listening to the false will that will only lead to the experience of inner destruction.

God's Will is rooted in perfection and equally shines on everyone. There is no favor in the Will of God.

God's Will is perfect peace and happiness and is found in the practice of true prayer. Being prayerful for a minute periodically throughout the day opens us to God's Will. The Will of God reaches us through quiet, peace and happiness.

The things I have always wished for have been for me alone. We are all conditioned by the carnal mind in the world to believe these things are normal. We may want to be married, have a home, kids, awesome job, money, great sex, influential friends, exotic vacations. When we are asking and wanting these things we are placing false gods before the the real God and creator of perfection.

When we turn our minds to God and feel the vibration of "thy Will be done not mine," things fall into place. Things not only fall into place, they come together in a way where no one loses.

God's will is a gentle, loving, happy vibe that is continuously flowing to all things. There is nothing here other than God. WE are collectively and personally blocking God's perfection with our little wants and needs.

Bad things happen and it's common in the world for the carnal mind to call it God's will. This is a false thought of great enormity. God's will is only perfection and it has no favor for anyone, or anything.

"31 Therefore do not worry, saying, 'What shall we eat?' or 'What shall we drink?' or 'What shall we wear?' 32 For the pagans pursue all these things, and your Heavenly Father knows that you need them. 33 But seek first the kingdom of God and His righteousness, and all these things will be added unto you." **Matthew**

One Voice

There is only one true Will, and there is also only one true Voice. The Voice for God governs the thinking in our minds if we are willing to allow it. You many wonder how this all comes back to food. Well it can't not come back to food. The compulsive voice that drives all compulsion wants us fat, sick and dead.

I have found the largest obstacle for me is recognizing when I am starting to listen to the voice of the serpent. It starts noticing stuff all around me that I don't like and find unacceptable. It (the thoughts in my mind) can sound spiritual and be very convincing to me, and whoever will listen. Unfortunately, I can sound very convincing! When I start listening to the serpent within, I am now measuring people's attitudes and motivations. I slowly start to feel BAD.

There is no change in anyone else's behavior that is going to "cure" me. Why is that? Because for every offensive action in the world observed and changed, there are a thousand more. It is a trap!

I have to roll back into my mind to the place where I took my first unnoticed wrong turn. Did someone not answer a question fast enough, or clear enough? This is a big serpent hook for me, not understanding what someone is saying. I get frustrated and start firing questions at them wanting them to clarify.

I was thinking this morning. "How can I possibly hear the bread of life coming from my brother when everyone is so messed up?" Danger! Danger! I have been experiencing terrible anxiety for a few days brought on by menopause? Poor thinking? All of the above. I saw it this morning in my thoughts. True prayer, is all about perceiving the kingdom. Listening to the One Voice and denying the rest. Deny. Deny. Deny the denial of Truth. In my OWN mind!

The more powerfully I am able to deny the denial of truth, the more I will bare witness to the miraculous. True prayer is all about denying the denial of truth.

T-12.II.1. Miracles are merely the translation of denial into truth. 2 If to love oneself is to heal oneself, those who are sick do not love themselves. 3 Therefore, they are asking for the love that would heal them, but which they are denying to themselves. 4 If they knew the truth about themselves they could not be sick. 5 The

task of the miracle worker thus becomes to deny the denial of truth. 6 The sick must heal themselves, for the truth is in them. 7 Yet having obscured it, the light in another mind must shine into theirs because that light is theirs.
A Course In Miracles

Temptation Always Leads To (Self) Judgment

Judgment is self-hatred and there is no exception in this. This is the Law of God. Being taught to "do unto others" is the key to freedom and peace, NOT a moral directive. When we judge another we feel the effects of that judgment through anxiety. We then want to eat, sleep and do anything we can to alleviate our anxiety. Anxiety is brought about by the projection of unconscious guilt and shame. Peace and radiance are attributes of innocence.

Think about it for a moment. When we succumb to the serpent's way in the pantry, we are then subject to all kinds of judgments of our own body. Next stop, anxiety and self-hatred. Remember, one of the ego's largest tools in its dark shed is forgetfulness. We slam someone verbally and have no clue why we feel TERRIBLE three days later.

My denial about carrying extra weight and what I was eating was HUGE. It was such an eye opening experience to eat when only hungry. That principle is THE END of denial.

Not giving into temptation is not always easy. However, the discomfort we feel from not leaning into temptation is much less than the effects of judgment. When someone is behaving from the place of guilt it is like a veil has come down. When we respond to it in any way, the veil comes down upon us as well. We are powerful in our ability to drop thought, whether it is appearing without or within.

Judgment brings us right into the hypnotism of the world. Our judgments of nothing are literally nothing, and being out of the care of God is the ONLY cause of anxiety. If you have ever suffered from anxiety or depression and have been healed, you KNOW this is so.

"One problem, one solution." A Course In Miracles

What is the problem? The carnal/ego thinking. What is the solution? Rising above through quiet and contemplation to the inspiration above.

I had terrible anxiety attacks and depression in my early twenties. I had all of the best treatment and doctors money can buy. I live in Boston where people travel the world to have access to the medical care I've had. At 21 years of age I had lost three years to this debilitating state of mind. What healed me? Walking under the desert sky with a quiet mind that knew there was something larger than myself healing me.

Going to shrink after shrink, and having my thinking within the realm of mortal mind examined, gave me MORE anxiety. I was practicing true prayer before I was even aware of what it was. The quiet under the desert night sky was leading me within myself. My first truly healing thought was this "if there is one being on this planet who has healed from this, I can too." I held fast to this thought and before you knew it, witnesses to this very thought began to appear. No more doctors! Moving in the sun, keeping the thought in place, caring for myself with exercise and nutrition began to turn the tide.

Judgement engages you in the dream of the world. There is no way around this. Believe in your judgments, you believe in the world, and that is a tough place to be. One does not need to resist any judgments, our true reality abides in gently looking beyond them. Judgment was never a moral issue. The master Jesus was teaching us not to have judgments in order to be free of the world. God is the everlasting vibe beneath all form. God is felt and experienced beyond our thinking mind.

When we are judgmental we are believing that we are bodies and that the thoughts we are telling ourselves are true. If we can draw back and see this all as the carnal mind, we begin to be free. The carnal mind is a non-stop judgmental machine that never turns off. It goes about convincing you that it is real, by continuously shooting its false thoughts into your mind. It begins to die off of neglect, as we withdraw belief in it.

There is a huge difference between being inspired, and moving about the world as a result of judgment. Using food as a place to develop this practice is an immeasurable gift. Who doesn't want an inspired life? Reaching into our higher mind for inspiration is a practice.

When I look back at my family history in the world, it is really tough. How can I ever make that right in my mind at the level of the world? The truth is that I can't, and you can't either. We can feel less-pain and resentment, but we can't get all the way to being free until we let go our false identity. This false identity is the carnal mind that has us convinced that it is us.

We are spirit bodies. We are eternal and are here right now animating the physical body. When any unhappy thoughts related to the body comes up we drop them and see them for what they are. This is the way to become free. I see my judgments for the nothingness that they are. The key is having the willingness. Once you believe that your thoughts are false, you can build a forward moving momentum towards happiness in the Garden of Eden. The Garden of Eden is a metaphor for The God-Vibe, which is up above the carnal mind within.

"My meaningless thoughts are showing me a meaningless world."
A Course In Miracles

All uninspired thought is meaningless, are we ready to let it all go? All uninspired thought, whether it APPEARS as good OR bad, is false. When we have suffered enough we will no doubt be ready to let go. I know personally I had to put in a lot of suffering, in order to let go.

Does this mean we will no longer enjoy a beautiful flower, or a cup of coffee? NO! It means we will approach all of those things from a deep place of reverence and appreciation instead of escape. That said, are you REALLY able to appreciate the fragrance and beauty of a flower when your mind is off of the rails? I know I look at them and feel I am not really seeing them when I am stuck outside of the gates of the Garden of Eden (higher mind).

Life Is Unmanageable Across The Board

The first step in Alcoholics Anonymous (AA) is the recognition that life has become unmanageable. It's true, we cannot go off of the rails within the realm of a thought system and then find relief within that same realm. AA is all about admitting one is powerless over addiction and then developing a relationship with a higher power. All true! There is no power in the carnal mind's thought system and the only answer is to rise above it to the God-Vibe.

When we have become so ensnared in the carnal mind, and we are carrying extra weight, things are sideways in more than just that area. My relationships suffered terribly because of my own thoughts of self-abasement. If I am unhappy about the way I look in my party dress, I will not be bringing my most shiny attitude to the party. This is not about vanity, it's about seeing the effects of listening to the voice of self-hatred. Eating for anything other than nourishment of the body is an act of self-hatred.

I could not tell how deeply into the thought system of self-hatred I was until I began to exit. The serpent within does NOT let go easily. It's not like you follow the principles and your life magically becomes the Garden of Eden and all of its perfection.

Right now wherever you are, consider this. Are you ready for your perfect mate? Are you ready for that awesome job and professional opportunity? If it's not already here, that is because we are not ready for it. We cannot have unmanageability in one area and shine in another.

It all comes back to a sense of worthiness and that is the last thing we are going to feel when we have been listening to the serpent's dictates. Its whole deal is to leave us feeling weak, shameful and broken down in any way it possibly can. Our feelings of shame and unworthiness breathe life into evil/ego.

When we begin to listen within around food, we then begin to listen within about everything. Often times people go on a diet, lose weight and their lives become chaotic in other areas. I have personally known a few people who have had lap band surgery and became very bad alcoholics. Some get slim and sexy and have affairs that destroy their marriages.

When someone says "I need to lose weight" it is a big fat lie. The only need is to reconnect with the

God-Vibe up above thought, in quiet. When we sit quietly in receptive mode, even for one minute a few times a day, things begin to shift around. We have made room for God and His works. In God there is no hurt, or harmfulness.

To judge yourself for having gained weight and then to go on a diet is paying penance for GUILT. Stop that.

Our lives becoming manageable again is not about control, it's about letting go of the reigns. This doesn't not mean to lay around like a zombie awaiting God to part the clouds. Oh no indeed, the inspired have more energy and inspiration than ever!

Get quiet within yourself and get rolling in a direction. It may be cleaning out a drawer, it may be walking on the Moon. That is all up to YOUR inner GPS (God, Prayers, Silence). You will know which way to go, remain receptive.

Prayer:

Thank you Father for in you I am made free.
Thank you Father for your unchangeable love
and perfection.

God's guidance never, ever leaves us. It is you and I who exit the Garden of our own will. There is no manageability in the carnal mind. The only way out of its anxiety is UP above the battle ground.

"See no one from the battleground, for there you look on him from nowhere. You have no reference point from where to look, where meaning can be given what you see. " A Course In Miracles

See no one and nothing from the reference point of the battle ground which is the carnal mind. Ask within BEFORE you eat, it only takes a moment of quiet and intention to listen.

This Too Shall Pass

Please remember this, when you are lifting your vibe above the carnal mind and out of hell, there IS resistance of GREAT magnitude. If you can go into this process knowing that, you will be prepared. How often do people throw in the towel when the going gets tough and uncomfortable? The answer is millions, every minute, of every day. What makes you any different? The simple truth that you now know. Rising above thought, not believing in judgments of yourself or others, sets you free.

What does this look like in everyday life? Letting go of temptations in thought is a mental exercise. One of the most insidious, entrapping thoughts are the thoughts of needing to lose weight. It is the same exact thing as having a bad marriage and thinking you need to get rid of your husband. There cannot be a "bad marriage," or an overweight body, without my thinking and therefore my actions making it so. Do you have resistance to these thoughts? Do we want to be right, or free of inner tyranny?

When I am no longer doing a mental tango with an image, where does the image go? When we cease our dance with dark thinking, the picture MUST change. For those of you who think I am saying stay in a "bad" relationship, that couldn't be further from the truth. If you have read my first book you will see that my doing a dance with the carnal mind put me right into layers of burning hell.

Let's go there shall we? When we stop doing our tango with the dark thinking of relationship, the relationship ends, or our partner rises to our Vision. It happens every day. Miracles are all about us, the one who holds the Vision WILL bare witness!

As well, when we stop our dance with thoughts of self-hatred that are tied into food and gluttony, our compulsion falls down. Why? It dies of neglect, we are literally no longer feeding it. If we fall off of the rails, we can instantly feel the dark vibe that has creeped back onto us. We drop those thoughts again and set our sight upon the Garden of Eden.

We Learn To Stop Harming Ourselves

Are we getting this yet? Learning to go beyond the carnal voice of compulsion is the beginning of seeing our self-harm. In what area of life have you harmed yourself and KNOW you are no longer going to do that to yourself again? If it was around money and you see yourself itching to use credit cards. "Oh, no" you may say to yourself "I'm NOT going there ever again." Then "see" that something is trying to take you down the road of self-destruction. Something is trying and that something is the carnal mind, also referred to as the serpent.

There are those who simply get into effects of the carnal mind and stop a behavior. They have not learned that the effects are coming from a cause that is invisible. When we don't address the cause of our ill-effects, they just bounce around, the pain and suffering will just change form.

Rare is the person who is able to stop self- harm and move to a lifted vibration without a lot of resistance. For most of us the lifting of our vibration is incremental. We literally need to be acclimated to feeling good.

Take a look around, everyone is practicing self-harm in some way. The hard part is breaking through our own wall of denial. Once we can see it, we begin the gentle process of unwinding. Being well aware of when we are practicing self -harm automatically begins its unraveling. Even if it is not apparent for some time, the seed of awareness has been planted.

In Conclusion-
There Is No Conclusion

This life and the lifting of one Soul's vibration is individual. That is what our real purpose is in life, to lift our vibration and reach out from a higher vibe to one another. Otherwise, we are just the blind leading the blind. We teach by demonstration. We teach by our attitudes in everyday life. We teach healing through our own healing words, deeds and attitudes. What is healing? The letting go of the carnal mind and its vicious desire to see us broken down, sickly and depressed.

"To teach is to demonstrate. 2 There are only two thought systems, and you demonstrate that you believe one or the other is true all the time. 3 From your demonstration others learn, and so do you. 4 The question is not whether you will teach, for in that there is no choice. " A Course In Miracles

Whenever I see someone overcome, I am so grateful because they are showing me my potential to overcome as well. We have such gifts to offer one another. We are continuously giving to those around us. We are choosing whether we are giving light by first receiving it ourselves, or giving darkness, sorrow and chaos.

I have seen the devastation of food addiction, and addictions of all kinds fall to the floor. Through the willingness to contemplate Truth and enter into the God-Vibe above the thinking mind, even for a minute per day, things begin to shift around.

Beneath the God-Vibe in the carnal thinking mind is where all things go wrong. Above the thinking mind is where Heaven and the Garden of Eden exist. They are still here, their reality has never changed. The God-Vibe is calling us back to the Garden.

To be continued....

True Prayer:

Thank you Father for you abide in me and I abide in you. The truth of who and what I am is your perfection. In you I am made whole and you would have me rest in your everlasting arms beneath all form. You straighten the crooked places with your spirit of love and abundance. Your bread of life is my only want and desire. The ground on which I sit, stand, lay, dance, run is sacred because you have made it so. Your bread of life flows freely to me from my brother. Your bread of life flows freely from me to my brother. Thank you Father. Thank you Father. Amen.

Lee Catalano is the Author of Breaking Spells: From Darkness To Light With A Course In Miracles; said to be the most intense application of *A Course In Miracles* ever written.

Lee has been a student of *A Course In Miracles* for 25 years. Along with being a student, she has also been ordained in the doctrine for 16 years.

"My family and I live by the belief that ONLY true prayer can set the Soul free from carnal tyranny."

Not only is her knowledge and understanding of *A Course In Miracles* stellar, her application is uncompromising.

Lee resides with her family of school teachers, therapists, students and mystics in Boston, Ma.

All speaking engagement inquires:
Revleecatalano@gmail.com

Made in the USA
Middletown, DE
23 February 2017